WHAT IS GENERIC HUMAN STUDIES?

Categorizing Human Reality and Experience Generically Speaking

John K. Pollard, III

Disclaimer: The information and procedures contained in this book are based on the personal research and professional experience of the author. The publishers present the information in this book for educational purposes only. It is not intended as a substitute for consulting with your physician or mental health care provider. The author and publishers are not responsible for any adverse affects or consequences resulting from the use of any of the suggestions, preparations, or procedures discussed in this book. A health care professional should supervise all matters pertaining to your health.

Published by

Generic Human Studies Publishing
9815 N. 95th Street, Scottsdale, AZ 85258 USA
Phone: 925-858-3137

Library of Congress Cataloging-in-Publication Data CIP Data Pending Publication Date July 2008

ISBN 0-942055-27-6

CONTENTS

Dedication

This book is dedicated to the ancient roots of our group humanity, which have grown through humanity's diversified past to create our current level of human expression.

Acknowledgments

Many wonderful and not-so-wonderful people have contributed to the creation of this book. In the interest of remaining generic, they shall remain unnamed.

FOREWORD

Dear Reader,

As a person who can heal any body, mind, or relational problem (within reason), this is the central groundwork of how I achieved this ability.

This book:

- Contains the core "DNA structure" of Generic Human Studies and represents a linear map through the system
- Takes the READER through a guided tour of its three major parts, but out of necessity is only an outline to its key elements
- Provides specific keys for any USER on a quest for deeper patterns of personal healing
- Is for the serious STUDENT of Generic Human Studies, embarking on a lifetime journey of investigation into their specific interests concerning the human body, mind and relations.
- Sets the standard for future works based on the knowledge of Generic Human Studies, some of which are already in print.

But first, perhaps I should define what I mean by Generic Human Studies;

I bid you welcome,

John K. Pollard, III
May 1, 2008

Chapter One:

What Is Generic Human Studies?

1. What is Generic Human Studies®? (GHS®)

Generic Human Studies (GHS®) is a codified information system (also called a "smart system") designed to help you, the USER, diagnose and resolve any difficult problems you are experiencing with your body, mind, and/or relations. GHS can help you in many ways, depending upon how you choose to use the system.

The GHS system presents a series of thinking algorithms similar to those designed in software programs called "smart systems." In the same way that computer programs can now beat chess grand-masters, the GHS system can often successfully "out-diagnose" medical practitioners and psychiatrists, as well as traditional religious or new age teachings.

GHS® is also a philosophy, a science, and an art. Philosophy is a system of thinking; science is the collection and codification of verifiable knowledge; art is the practitioner's skill in applying the philosophy and science of a system to everyday human problems.

The GHS® System is designed to facilitate the healing of the body, mind, and/or relations. The more you accept the philosophy, study the science and apply the art of Generic Human Studies®, the more deeply you will be able to use the system on a personal or "USER-level" basis.

2. WHY USE THE TERM "GENERIC"?

The word generic describes a basic product or idea without a trademark or brand name. This term can also describe the fundamental characteristics of a person, place, or thing. A collection of common characteristics is considered "generic" to that person, place, or thing.

For example, a generic car has:

- Four wheels
- An engine
- Brakes
- A steering wheel
- Etc.

If you put the collection of common characteristics together what do you have? You have a generic car.

On the other hand, a Lexus automobile also has:

- Four wheels
- An engine
- Brakes
- A steering wheel

However, the Lexus is seen as different from a generic car in many ways:

- A 12 speaker interior sound system
- Advanced ergonomic styling
- Japanese craftsmanship, luxury leather seats
- Etc.

The differences between non-generic cars can be many and varied. They may involve key components or superficial attributes. Yet if you look at the generic attributes of all cars, no matter how different they may be from each other, they will still contain the generic attributes any car must have to remain a car.

In Generic Human Studies, we use the word generic to ensure any aspects of our information system will apply to all human beings. What we teach is defined as applying to all humans regardless of culture, religion, or politics.

3. But the Term "Generic" Has a Negative Connotation.

The word "generic" is considered negative only when the general public doesn't yet understand the use of the term as it relates to indentifying human problems.

When they do understand the connection, the term generic is considered positive and people enthusiastically embrace the term.

Perhaps you have heard the phrase, "principles before personalities"? GHS defines "principles" as the generic truth of information versus the "personality" of the human being teaching the information.

In today's popular culture people are often so impressed by the messenger, they are completely oblivious to the weak or pointless information he or she is presenting.

4. How Can You Use the Term Generic When Describing Human Beings?

GHS strives to codify knowledge and make it accessible to all. Various individuals and groups have isolated and described generic principles in the fields of body-work, mind-work, and/or relation-work using their own brand name terminology.

Many of these ideas are excellent, yet these people and groups often charge exorbitant fees or require unreasonable amounts of time to study their ideas or teachings.

Most teachers, workshops, and "spiritual" groups teach essentially the same principles using different names, procedures, or outlines. Yet their issues, concepts, or information are identical to the generic perspective.

Typically these teachings remain provincial, with limited viewpoints that become the center of their observations, rather than a window to the generic whole.

A few of these groups proclaim their brand-name version of generic information as different, unique, or the only source of knowledge, when in fact many of these systems are direct spin-offs or rip-offs of previously known systems.

5. Why Use the Term "Human"?

The term "Human" is used because Generic Human Studies is about humans. All the information in Generic Human Studies applies to each of the individual members of any human society whether past, present, or future.

Every concept in GHS is universal to all humans at a similar stage of development. Despite the many cultures, religious and political systems shaped by humanity, every human being has a similar body, mind, and relations, if you can recognize this from the level of Generic Human Studies.

Learning the GHS information system is to learn what similarities all humans share, rather than to concentrate on the external differences separating us.

6. Why Use the Term "Studies"?

The term "Studies" is used because this "brand name" of knowledge (Generic Human Studies®) is a body of knowledge that must be studied through reading, observation, and practical application to be understood.

The GHS Information System, though simple to traverse, has many deeper and more advanced layers of information. To understand its breadth and depth would take years. To use GHS to seek practical benefit for a problem in your life could take minutes.

7. How Does Generic Human Studies Make Things Easier?

Each category of human knowledge has commonly accepted principles that are known, taught, and learned by those who study in that particular field. In the same way that individual human cultures may have a different term and description for the concept of "gravity" in relation to of their current level of understanding (medicine man, priest, scientist), humans have managed to develop a confusing array of brand name descriptions for generic principles and experiences common to all human beings.

In the same way the study of physics describes, catalogues, and teaches the principles of physical matter, GHS concerns itself with the principles of human function and interaction.

We are all human; we all have common needs. It is time for us to face this reality and start helping each other to grow toward the meeting of our generic needs.

There is no longer any need for one "guru" or "philosophy" professing the reality of life to fight with another "guru" or "philosophy", unless they themselves do not understand the GHS principles connecting humanity.

GHS gives people a language that can be understood by everyone. It is not difficult to comprehend, nor is it totally simplistic either.

GHS can be as complex as humanity itself. By starting with what is already generically known, you have a sound foundation upon which to pursue further study.

8. Why Do We Need Generic Human Studies?

Why can't humans be satisfied with what we already know and accept? Why do we need a new system with yet another explanation of how life works?

Because GHS connects these systems together in the same way as the trunk of a tree connects the branches with its roots.

Once you understand the roots of Generic Human Studies you will be at the core of what you want to know. As a result you will know where to go for more information in your specific area of interest.

The GHS information system begins to evaluate the human experience on its core level. Think about it; there are many more similarities to humans than there are differences.

Doesn't an Arab's face have two eyes in almost the same place as a Jewish face? Don't Chinese have the same basic body structure as Africans? There may be some superficial differences, but how is it that all the diverse races of man have only produced two sexes in similar sizes, with identical organs and body parts? Why isn't one set of humans 30 feet tall, and another less than 10 inches?

9. What is a Founding Principle of Generic Human Studies?

By observing and categorizing conditions common to all humans, the GHS information system approaches human knowledge as generic in scope, rather than limited by a specific culture, religion or political system.

We don't strip away the cultural, religious, or political variations of the human experience; we just put them where they belong, external to the generic realities of human existence.

GHS is a deep well, drilled down to the bedrock truth of humanity. It defines a new standard for the study of human potential.

Rather than give a common human condition or an attribute a brand name or label, the GHS information system has distilled the concepts of human potential to a generic core, making the evaluation and solving of human problems simpler and easier.

If it wouldn't be true for "cave men" 10,000 years ago, then it's not true for GHS today. Any insight of GHS referring to the Body, Mind, or Relations has to be true for all of humanity's existence.

10. WHAT IS THE PURPOSE OF GENERIC HUMAN STUDIES?

The purpose of Generic Human Studies is to provide training for students and teachers who want to help themselves and others increase the enjoyment and experience of their lives.

The initial focus of the GHS Smart System is to give the student/practitioner an organized way to learn more about the problem area in which he/she is interested.

For additional studies, many outside books/tapes/videos are referenced (or not) in their appropriate place for further information.

Our base of accumulated knowledge defines and expands the core knowledge of the three human concerns without using brand names, cult concepts, or personalized labels and with no exclusionary policies.

11. What is the Guiding Philosophy of Generic Human Studies?

GHS has the following guiding principles:

We are all human, and we all have needs. GHS says it is time to admit this to ourselves individually and collectively. We must begin learning to help each other fulfill our mutual needs. The end product and goal of GHS is for each human to be capable of self-providing his or her own personal needs.

Human beings achieve happiness by helping others fulfill their needs. Human needs are generic in that we each have essentially the same desires. Although each society shapes and colors those of its members with a cultural and socialized version, all humans have the same generic needs.

As the personal needs of one human become fulfilled, it is a natural extension for him or her to want to help other humans meet their own. As a result, fulfilled and happy humans can help other unfulfilled and unhappy people to improve their life-experience.

A successful outcome of GHS principles would be for more individuals to carry the equivalent of their own weight in life by not consuming the resources of others without contributing energies in return.

CHAPTER TWO:

WHO WANTS GENERIC HUMAN STUDIES?

12. Who Would Want to Use the GHS System?

Anyone who has or wants to evaluate and/or fix a major body, mind, or relational problem will want to utilize the GHS Smart System.

The first step is to evaluate the problem in a comprehensive manner, in order to have a clear idea of what the problem is and the specific location of the problem.

Next, you follow the generic steps to fix the problem yourself or have it fixed.

13. WHO ARE YOU, THE USER?

You, the USER, are a person with a major life problem.

Since you are responsible for your life, you are the most likely person to know all the details about your problem. Therefore, you are the best person to make an informed choice of how you want to proceed to solve this or any life problem you might be experiencing. Plus, you are the one with the most to gain from a successful resolution of your problem.

The Generic Human Studies Smart System was created so you can have an informed approach to solving any problem you might have involving your:

- Body
- Mind
- Relations

Using GHS, you can make certain you manage the solution of your problem in the best possible manner.

14. WHY SHOULD I, THE USER, CARE ABOUT GHS?

GHS is designed to help you, the USER.

It is about you, your life, and what you've got going on, generically speaking.

If you want to improve some aspect of your body, mind, or relations, then you owe it to yourself to investigate the GHS smart-system to see what it can do for you.

The most important reason you should care about GHS is it will help you diagnose and correct whatever problem you are having in your life right now, for which you are getting no help or answers from other sources.

15. HOW DOES IT WORK?

Let us assume you have a major body, mind, or relational problem that you want to evaluate and/or fix. The GHS Smart System takes you through a series of questions.

Simply by following the sequence of questions and going to the next applicable level, you bring clarity, and understanding to your problem. It is especially valuable in difficult or baffling problem areas.

You solve the problem by using the GHS Smart System to choose a series of personal action steps based on the generic probabilities.

Your life has three basic problem areas. Every problem you are concerned with right now originates from one (or a combination) of these areas:

- Your Body
- Your Mind
- Your Relations

Using the GHS information system you can work out the best probabilities to:

- Pinpoint the exact area causing the problem
- Evaluate your problem comprehensively
- Fix your problem once you know what is wrong, or be advised where to go for help

16. What Good is Using the GHS System?

Using the GHS Smart System for solving problems gives you immediate skills and power for solving life's problems. First you form a diagnosis of what is wrong, and then you go for appropriate help.

Before GHS, your ability to evaluate the cause and fix a problem in your life was relegated to expensive professional consultations. If you were lucky and your problem was extremely obvious or common, you might have been given some answers.

Once you begin working with Generic Human Studies Smart System, you will find it impossible to go back to anything less advanced. Its purpose is to give you, the individual, specific keys and insights to focus on solving your personal problems.

17. Why is GHS So Effective?

GHS is so effective because it brings what was exclusively professional knowledge in the past to a layman's level today.

So much knowledge has been accumulated and disseminated to the public that often a person with a specific problem knows as much about it as a qualified professional in that field.

Unfortunately, many of today's professionals haven't caught up with what's available on a lay level today in areas outside their specialty. Therefore, they can be in the dark when it comes to helping someone correct an unusual set of symptoms or circumstances.

Also, if the USER has a problem, he or she is motivated to seek a solution. If they are not hampered by a rigid belief system, they might be willing to look at any possible solution that could rationally explain their problem.

Since GHS has sought the generic information in each generic category, we offer the generic solution for each problem area, possibly unfamiliar to professional practitioners outside this area.

18. WHO DECIDES WHAT THE PROBLEM IS?

Each person decides where he or she believes the source problem might be. Then one proceeds to try and solve the problem. Once the potential cause or source of your problem is diagnosed, help can be obtained more successfully.

Generic Human Studies can advise you of specific practitioners and ways to help, based on the problems you present during the GHS Interview. You then choose which course to take.

19. To Whom Should Generic Human Studies® (GHS) Appeal?

The teachings and principles of Generic Human Studies should appeal to people with positive and concrete learning experiences associated with at least ten of the following teachers or disciplines.

The more practical experience you have with disciplines of this nature, the more beneficial value you will receive from GHS.

20. Body Work Practitioners

Patients and practitioners of the following bodywork systems: (Listed in alphabetical order, not in order of importance)

- Alexander
- Chiropractic
- Feldenkrais
- Hellerwork
- Massage
- Physical Therapy
- Rolfing
- Yoga

21. Mind Work Practitioners

If it were possible to completely understand Generic Human Studies, here is a partial sampling of the consciousness growth teachers who would be important to know for various reasons. (Listed in alphabetical order, not in order of importance)

- Barbara DiAngeles
- Buddhism
- Buckminster Fuller
- Dale Carnegie
- Ernest Holmes
- Guru Maharaji
- Hinduism
- John Bradshaw
- John-Rodger
- José Silva
- Ken Keyes
- Krishnamurti
- L. Ron Hubbard
- Louise Hay
- Maharishi Mahesh Yogi
- Marianne Williamson
- Moshe Feldenkrais
- Parmahansa Yoganada
- Rev. Schuller
- Robert Orr
- Sai Baba
- Sat Chit Ananda
- Shakti Gawain
- Shirley McClaine
- Sondra Ray
- Taoism
- Thomas Gordon
- Tim Gallway
- Werner Erhard
- Yogi Bajan

22. RELATION WORK PRACTITIONERS

People who have taken, studied, and benefited from the following: (Listed in alphabetical order, not order of importance)

- Actualizations
- Adult Children of Alcoholics
- EST/The Forum
- Huna as taught by Max Freedom Long
- Insight
- Life-Spring
- Living Love
- LRT
- Making Love Work
- MSIA
- Rebirthing
- Scientology
- Self-Esteem Workshops
- SELF-PARENTING Program
- Self-Realization Fellowship
- Silva Mind Control
- Transcendental Meditation

23. How Could Generic Human Studies Help Me Specifically?

Each student picks the area in GHS he/she wants to study first. Typically, this is the area in which he/she has a crisis situation or a strong interest.

GHS helps the sincere student to access this body of knowledge to improve the specific problems in his/her life.

The more a person knows about each of the generic areas of concern in his/her life, the better he or she is able to solve the types of problems he/she encounters in this world.

24. What Has Generic Human Studies Done?

Generic Human Studies has developed and cataloged knowledge in the three areas of body, mind, and relations so students may study these areas and bring its value into the decision-making process of their lives.

Both Lay and Practitioner Students learn simple and practical ways to apply this information to the improvement of their physical health, mental/emotional happiness, and/or their relational interactions.

25. What's My Next Step?

If you want to learn more about the Generic Human Studies information system, you need to continue to read and understand the GHS information presented about your body, mind, and relations.

This is accomplished by concentrating on what are called the "three areas of concern" in GHS.

Chapter Three:

What Are the Three Areas of Concern?

26. WHAT ARE THE THREE CONCERNS IN GHS?

Generic Human Studies has categorized its collection of knowledge into three areas of human life.

Reduced down to its simplest essence, human life consists of three basic areas of concern:

- Your Body
- Your Mind
- Your Relations

27. Why Do We Need the Three Areas of Concern?

Everything that is personally bothering you in your life, *really* bothering you, is caused by a problem in one (or more) of three areas. If you are seeking a solution to a non-specific problem, the sooner you can isolate and evaluate its exact cause, the sooner you can begin to seek and create a solution.

Too many people are suffering from undiagnosed, yet generic, problems of which they are simply unaware. Even an expert in one problem area might not realize the cause of your symptoms if it originates from another area.

For example, you might go to a mind specialist when you have a body problem (such as headaches), or a body specialist for a health problem caused by a relation problem (bad marriage).

This is made even more confusing by the fact that many times a problem in your body, mind, or relation can cause a symptomatic flare up in another area. This secondary symptom in the other area may be the first time your problem has attracted the attention of your conscious mind.

Most experts can hardly be called experts if you take a serious look at what they don't know. Specialists often know so little in the areas outside the field of their expertise; they are virtually idiot savants of no use to the generic human for truly helping them sort out a complicated problem.

28. What is the Reality of Solving Your Problems?

Let me make one point perfectly clear.

If you want to solve a serious problem in your life, you will have to manage and be concerned about the solution to this problem yourself.

You may require lots of outside assistance, but you are the one that will have to be responsible for asking the questions that guide the process and following through on the time, energy, and commitment necessary to solve the problem.

Why? Because you are the one who cares the most. After all, you are the one suffering from the problem and its impact on your life.

29. How Can You Relegate All Of Humanity Into Three Areas of Concern?

Whatever problem you have with a computer, there can be only one (or a combination) of three potential causes:

Hardware: There is something wrong with the physical workings of the computer: the disc drive, the cable, the monitor, etc. Once the hardware problem is diagnosed and repaired, the problem is solved. Now the computer works properly again.

Software: All computers require software to initialize and run the hardware. If there is a software "bug", the computer will malfunction in strange and bewildering ways. Once the software is repaired, upgraded, or changed, the computer can now run the way it is supposed to run.

Network: If one computer needs to interact with another computer, which is certainly part of what makes computers useful, a network is needed for this purpose. Both computers may be fine on their own, but the connection between the two can be faulty. Once the cause of the network problem is discovered and fixed, then the computers will communicate properly.

30. What Are Some Wrong Answers People Try to Break the Computer Analogy?

I've used this analogy for 22 years in every field of endeavor, including with computer professionals. Two early answers that people initially suggest are things that can go wrong with computers are the User, and no electricity.

The User: If it is the User, and "putting white-out on the computer screen to edit a document" is one such example, then this is a User problem; not a computer problem. The computer is fine in and of itself.

Electricity: If there is no power or electricity in this case, then this is an "electricity" problem. IF there was power, the computer would work fine.

In GHS the "electricity" is life-force energy provided by being alive. If you are not alive then GHS won't help you.

31. How Can You Compare a Computer to a Human?

In the same way the study of fixing computers (a vast and complicated body of knowledge) can be divided into three areas of concern (Hardware, Software, Network), so the study of humans can be categorized into three areas of concern (Body, Mind, Relations).

By use of this computer analogy, humans also have three major categories where problems can occur. In a similar manner, they are hardware, software, and networking problems, which we term body, mind, or relational problems.

When the correct diagnosis and treatment is found in the specific area causing the problem, then the problems go away and the human can once again "function" happily as he/she was designed to do.

32. How Does GHS Help With the Body?

Are you in pain? Is one or more of your joints or extremities hurt in a way that doesn't seem to go away? Do you have unexplained physical symptoms for which you are getting no decent resolution?

There are three areas of the physical body (hardware) that can be causative to many other problems. They are:

- The Skeletal System
- The Digestive System
- The Hormonal System

By bringing your focus to each of these systems, you can evaluate body symptoms and problems. The skeletal, digestive, and hormonal systems each have generic signs and symptoms.

By comparing your symptoms to the generic standard, you can determine if you find a match. When you can determine which one of these body systems is causing your problem, then you can go to the appropriate person or discipline to see what can done about it.

33. HOW DOES GHS SPECIFICALLY HELP THE BODY?

GHS teaches a unique form of bodywork and exercise that can restore normal motion and flexibility to your Skeletal System, giving you results you can see and feel. Called Articular Therapy, this system is practiced by Chiropractors and Massage Therapists who have taken this training.

GHS teaches the USER how to understand and evaluate his/her Digestive System so he or she can seek the proper approach to solving digestive type problems. The lay source for this understanding is explained in the book, *The Digestive Awareness Diet: You Are HOW You Eat.*

The Hormonal System creates a multitude of health problems, usually after chronic breakdown of the Skeletal and Digestive Systems. With proper testing and evaluation many problems can be solved in this area, problems that impact many other areas such as the mind or relations.

Using the GHS protocols to determine where to put your best efforts and time will save you time, money, and suffering.

34. How Does GHS Help With the Mind?

Are you confused? Do you have Inner Conflicts? Are you not where you know you ought to be or could be mentally? Does one part of your mind want to do one thing while another part wants to do the exact opposite?

GHS presents a unique and original system for understanding your mind and how it functions. Our system has been adopted by therapists and teachers around the world.

Known by its trade name The SELF-PARENTING Program, this system of understanding the function of the mind creates breakthroughs in understanding that continue to be unreachable using any other thinking or consciousness-growth system including the copies and fakes.

There is no mental system with a more extensive knowledge of how the mind works than the SELF-PARENTING Program.

35. How Does GHS Help With Relations?

Are you aware of how much the quality of your daily experiences revolve around your personal outer relations? Do you realize how many of your personal daily needs are fulfilled by your relations?

Generic Human Studies has pioneered an unparalleled understanding of the dynamics of relations. We can teach you the anatomy of relations and how to understand and repair your relational problems.

Because a relation takes place between two humans, unfortunately, one person in the relation cannot necessarily solve a true relational problem.

However, one person can evaluate a relation and decide if it's possible or desirable to solve a relational problem. The lay source for this understanding is explained in the book, *How Relationships Work: Introducing the Playground Analogy of Relationships.*

If both humans work on a relational problem using the knowledge of generic human studies, than it easily has the potential to be solved.

Chapter Four:

What Is GHS Body Work?

36. WHAT IS THE GENERIC HUMAN BODY?

Think of your body as hardware.

Your body's physical bones, organs, and flesh functions similarly, though not identically, to computer hardware. Your body is composed of physical and mechanical parts that are interconnected by an electrical system. If the physical parts are broken or incomplete in some way, the system simply will not work.

To make an obvious point, if you have a hole in your heart, one leg missing, or a damaged liver, then your body will have mechanical problems.

More to the point, the stress of daily living causes various internal parts to wear unevenly, break down, or become inoperable for various reasons. These changes are often subtle and occur over time.

You become aware of most physical problems only after your body has gone into an advanced state of disrepair and it begins to send you symptoms.

Another possibility is that you have been functioning fine and then something traumatic happens. You have a fall or an accident, or eat some toxic chemicals, or have some other type of unusual occurrence.

After this time, even though the problem originated some time earlier, you are still having symptoms past the point of "normal." If you just go through the "normal" ways of treating symptoms, you may find yourself soon out of options.

37. What are the Three Important Parts of the Generic Human Body?

Three hardware subsystems act together to control the optimal balance of health in the body: These subsystems are causative to the rest of the body's functions (as far as human intervention goes):

- Skeletal: for structural support, movement and to protect the nervous system and internal organs
- Digestive: for maintenance and repair to supply ongoing energy and repair to the body's cells and organs
- Hormonal: for short-term, and long-term organ and energy regulation

Additional subsystems exist in the body of course, but they are secondary to the three systems mentioned above.

Each of the three major systems works in conjunction to control and regulate the other subsystems.

If the three systems above were functioning correctly, it would be very difficult for other parts of the body hardware to break down or malfunction, barring poisoning or accidents.

Chapter Five:

What Is Deeper Look at the Skeleton?

38. WHAT DOES THE SKELETAL SYSTEM DO?

Your skeleton provides the mechanical frame of your body hardware, and is intimately connected to all body functions. The skeletal system is the first system to investigate in Generic Human Studies in order to resolve a wide variety of common, yet not commonly understood, symptoms in the body.

It is instrumental to all physical movements, large and small. It supports and protects the internal organs. It also protects and provides the distribution channel for the body's electrical system (the nerves), which provides the communication network between the brain, the internal/external organs, and the outside world.

If your skeleton is not working "normally", then you can have joint pains, internal organ problems, allergies, headaches and all kinds of symptoms that may never appear to be skeletal in origin.

39. Why Are Joints Important to the Skeleton?

The importance of joints is they are the key factor that enables the skeleton to move. The skeleton is basically a collection of bones that are lashed together by fascia and enclosed together with organs, muscles, and nerves in a watery sack.

It's the specific functionality of the joints that provides for the support for the internal body's structure as well as creating the potential for movement.

- The skeleton's first major role is weight-bearing.
- Its second major purpose is to enable movement.

40. How Do Joints Facilitate Movement?

Joints allow movements in different directions according to their structural mechanics. The direction and distance than each joint can typically move is called its range of motion.

Each joint in the body has an ideal "range of motion" based on how the joint links the two bones together. It is the joint's range of motion that determines how freely it can move. If all the joints enjoy their ideal range of motion, then the skeleton will have its best chance to move as it was designed.

Each joint has an allowable range of movement which leads to three classifications of articulations:

- Immovable
- Slightly movable
- Freely movable

Articular Therapy is primarily concerned with the freely movable joints. However, there are even nuances to this discussion as freely movable joints have three ranges of motion. The third range of motion is what is missing in the knowledge bank of the majority of bodywork practitioners.

41. What Are the Three Primary "Ranges of Motion" of Movable Joints In the Skelton?

Each movable joint has three normal ranges of motion. They are:

Active Range:

The range of motion a person can initiate using his or her own power. (Average people know about this.)

Passive Range:

The range of motion a second person can put the joint through without the first person helping. Passive range is usually greater than active range of motion. (Most professional practitioners know about this.)

Joint Play:

Joint Play is a specific micro-movement between the articulating bones within the joint capsule only. The joint capsule is a covering that completely surrounds each joint so the lubricating liquid within the joint will not escape.

A trained examiner using a specific method of palpation can test for this movement. (Most professional bodywork practitioners are NOT aware of this nor do they know how to test for it.)

42. Why Is the Unknown Aspect of "Joint Play" So Important In the Skelton?

Joint play is a crucial movement for the integrity of a joint as it is the precursor movement for both passive and active ranges of motion. When a joint loses its joint play movement through trauma or disease, it is not possible to regain the lost joint play through exercise or other passive therapies.

A person can't "feel" if his/her own joint play is restricted. When the two bones cannot make this micro-movement within their capsule, the rest of the larger movements of the joint are forced to "go around" this micro fixation, and this alters the physics of their normal movement.

Unless a practitioner knows how to find and fix missing joint play, then there is no way for the joint to regain its normal function. Rest and/or exercise are useless.

43. What Happens When "Joint Play" Becomes Restricted?

As a joint in the body starts to lose (its internal joint play) range of motion, it becomes what is known as "fixated." This means there is a loss of normal range of motion between the two surfaces of the opposing joints. A joint can have various degrees of fixation, from slight, moderate, major, all the way to complete fixation.

This fixation typically starts within the joint capsule through a fall or injury. Once a joint becomes compromised on this micro level, the effect of missing joint play affects the macro-movement of the joint, typically creating symptoms in the opposite or related joint.

Once the attention of the USER or a health practitioner becomes focused on the symptom side, there's no hope for correcting the cause, and the treatment prognosis goes down from there.

It's imperative when treating joint dysfunction to seek the original cause of the problem, typically a fixated joint. This saves everyone the frustration of experiencing and treating symptoms which cannot be corrected on the level of the symptom.

44. WHAT PROBLEMS DO "FIXATIONS" CAUSE WITHIN THE SKELETON?

Once a joint becomes "fixated" it loses its lubricating function inside the joint capsule, which causes it to become even drier and more immobile. Now the rest of the joints in the skeleton have to compensate by moving more or simply adapting to the fixated joint as best they can within the limitations of the self-enclosed system.

Based on the mechanical problems in the spine and skeleton creating symptoms of various kinds, it can be fairly stated that there is no symptom that can't be caused by articular dysfunction.

45. How Do "Fixated joints" Create Problems in the Body that the Users can Feel?

The interesting thing about a fixated joint is that you can't feel it. Since it is not moving, there is nothing to feel. The tiny nerves surrounding the joint (know as the *Proprioreceptors*) are no longer being stimulated, so there is no pain to detect.

What does happen, and this is the key point of this discussion, is that the opposing joint (a previously normal joint) begins to adapt to the fixation by moving *more* within its joint capsule. This problem begins to grow until it is termed a "hyper-mobile" joint.

For example, an ankle fixated on the left side can cause a (hyper-mobile) symptomatic flare-up in the right ankle, or the left knee. A fixated shoulder on the right side can cause an elbow/wrist problem on the right side, or a sore shoulder on the left.

Because this adaptive movement is forcing the capsule of the normal joint to extend beyond its range of allowance, it DOES trigger the proprioreceptors and other nerves and muscles surrounding the joint. This causes tearing, swelling, and pain, within the joint structures and as a set of symptom usually gains the attention of the USER quite noticeably.

When the person first experiences these symptoms they think they "popped a knee" or "strained their shoulder." They only know what their symptom feels like and what they were doing at the time. They have no idea that the true cause of their problem was already in place and was an accident waiting to happen.

46. WHAT IS THE PROBLEM WITH "FIXATED JOINTS" AS FAR AS THE USER IS CONCERNED?

Fixated joints don't hurt. So the USER would never go to a medical professional to have this problem corrected.

However, the opposing joint of a fixation, typically the same joint on the other side, or the next joint away from the fixated joint, does experience pain, and it can be quite painful.

The problem is that the pain side, the inflamed joint side, is the SYMPTOM. It's a typically normal joint that's being over-stretched and aggravated due to the fixated joint somewhere else. The CAUSE is the fixated joint which doesn't hurt at all.

Perhaps you have experienced this as a client. If you take your sore right shoulder to a Chiropractor, Osteopath, Physiotherapist, Doctor, Specialist, Orthopedic Surgeon, Neurologist, for an adjustment, massage, ultrasound, X-ray, MRI, operation, etc, it will be your right shoulder that gets all the adjusting, prodding, poking, sticking, zapping and cutting.

The other side, the fixated articulation causing all the trouble in the first place, is blissfully ignored by all because it is asymptomatic. Occasionally treating the sore side helps the pain a bit but it can also make the already hyper-mobile side symptomatically worse.

Rest is often medically prescribed for such an injury. All that does is allow the joint to recover until the pain goes away. Once you resume your normal activities, the problem returns.

47. What Internal Force Controls the Overall System of Joint Function?

Tensegrity (a combination of the words tension & integrity) is the construction principle used by nature to distribute tensional stress continuously throughout all parts of a structure. This word was coined by Buckminster Fuller (American architect and inventor of the Geodesic Dome among other things) to explain the way that nature builds structures.

We are not made up of stacks of blocks resting securely one on top of another, but rather a system of interlocking poles and guy wires. Tensegrity is nature's favorite device for achieving maximum stability with a minimum of material. This function of Tensegrity in the human body acts like an internal force of mechanical homeostasis. It always seeks the most balanced distribution between the stresses of the struts and guy wires.

When a fixation in the body is reversed through Articular Therapy, Tensegrity takes over the task of internal repair and reconstruction by altering the rest of the body's fascia to move and adapt to its new freedom.

Even after years of mechanical fixation, new movement in the body articulations can respond miraculously through the action of tensegrity. I've proven this over and over.

48. WHAT IS AN EXAMPLE OF TENSEGRITY?

The kite is a simple, realistic example of a structure utilizing tensegrity. A kite is made up of sticks, elastic bands (or string), and a tensed sheet of plastic or paper. If these individual pieces are just piled together on the ground then nothing fancy happens.

However, if you place the sticks inside the strings creating a tensional force and wrap this structure with tensed paper, it becomes light enough yet strong enough to fly in a strong wind without breaking apart. It is the tension between the sticks pulling on the guy wires of the string that holds the kite together.

There are also toy kits that come with struts and bands from which you can create your own tensegrity models.

49. How Does Tensegrity Work In the Body?

Your body is a primary example of nature's greatest tensegrity structure. In your body, tensegrity is a force that monitors and distributes tension between all dimensions of the skeleton, the muscles and the connective tissues (also called fascia).

The bones in the body act as spacer bars. The muscles and ligaments act as the tensional forces. The fascia is the broad sheets of binding material that hold the organs, nerves and muscles in place.

It is through the dynamics of tensegrity that our body is able to move, bend and withstand the amount of stress and strain that it does.

50. How Does Tensegrity Impact the Work of Articular Therapy?

Each person's body holds an accumulated total of tensegrity tension that is calibrated in exact response to the amount and type of tensional stress created by the joint fixations their body has incurred. The degree to which tensegrity distributes tensions between his/her various fixated joints will determine the degree to which a client feels "out of place."

Typically a person doesn't feel "out of place" until tensegrity tension has "way" surpassed allowable limits. There is a built-in allowance factor that enables a wide variety and range of stressors to impact the body. When stress points pass these allowable limits it creates symptoms. Tensegrity can then shift and redistribute tension and pressure to less vulnerable areas and the symptoms go away. However there is a cost of reduced function for the overall system.

This is how problems "you used to have" can go away symptom-wise, but from that point on your body has a severe reduction in the totality of what you used to be able to achieve, mechanically speaking. Consciously you think your problem is gone. In reality, your problem has just become chronic, and your body just turned off the alarm signals as a function of survival.

51. What Is the Approach of Articular Therapy with Regards to Tensegirty?

The approach of Articular Therapy is to seek the joint with the greatest restriction and loosen this first. Then the body's natural ability to redistribute tensegrity tension will bring back the ease and comfort to articular movement that every client seeks.

A person typically has two to three joints that are causing problems for all the others in terms of movement and tensegrity. Just loosening the tightest joint typically brings immediate symptomatic relief.

Articular symptoms in the body are the last thing to show up and the first thing to go away. Getting rid of symptoms is easy. Restoring damaged articular structures takes work but is achievable.

Part of the joy of being an Articular Therapy practitioner is to witness the magical workings of tensegrity as genuinely fixated and dysfunctional limbs begin to restore themselves right beneath your fingers.

52. What Are the key Joints of the Skeleton?

All parts of the skeleton are important of course, but the question might be asked, "If the skeleton is a walking cage, what are the key joints of skeletal movement?" In other words, if the skeleton was to move with optimum ease, based on its mechanical structure, what are the primary joints that facilitate movement?

From the Generic Human Bodywork point of view, the key movable joints are:

- The Ankles
- The Hips
- The Shoulders
- The Spine

53. Why Are the Ankles Important in Generic Human Bodywork?

The ankles have two important functions that control body movement. The first is the ankles are the transfer point between the ground and the rest of the body. Your total weight is supported and transferred through the two (L/R) ankle bones called the talus.

Everybody's feet have to touch the ground. The proper balance of the foot and ankle is the foundation for all subsequent acts of skeletal mobility.

Another important principle of AT is that restoring ankle movements is critical for fixing the knees and hips. By treating the ankle and having the USER continue performing their articular exercises, he/she will get the fastest possible response time to correcting lower extremity problems.

The most objective standard for treating whole body articular problems begins with mobilizing the ankles.

54. Why Are the Hips Important in Generic Human Bodywork?

The hips form the base or foundation for the lower back. If the hips are balanced and moving freely, it is almost impossible for something to go wrong mechanically with the lumbar spine. If your hips are fixated you would be walking like the Tin Man in the Wizard of Oz.

It's also important to note, the same Cause/Symptom dichotomy exists in this area as well. If your left lower back is chronically in spasm, it's probably the left side hip that is fixated, or perhaps the right side, depending on the pull of tensegrity. As the hips are in the middle of the tensegrity cage, they can create symptoms above, below, and across from the side of the fixation.

It's amazing how my people are functionally limping due to one hip socket being fixated more than the other. This progression happens so slowly the USER has no idea of his/her dysfunction, even when pointed out by others. I call it the "Grandpa McCoy" syndrome.

55. Why Are the Shoulders Important in Generic Human Bodywork?

Articularly speaking, the neck is resting upon and between the articular tensions of the shoulders. If there is a moderate fixation (or more) in the either shoulder, the neck cannot rest comfortably on its articular foundation.

Joint movements by the USER with a fixated shoulder will mandate that the neck be held uncomfortably. Also, the shoulders are the primary joints which anchor all manner of upper extremity movements.

As a silently fixated shoulder on the left starts aggravating the right shoulder, the USER will find themselves throwing, lifting, golfing, etc, in a manner that is different to their normal. As they start to alter their "normal" pattern to compensate for their pain, shoulder fixations will eventually affect them in more obvious ways.

56. Why Is the Spine Important in Generic Human Bodywork?

The spine is the center pole supporting the "inside" of the tensegrity cage. It is like the main pole holding up the rest of a circus tent. It consists of 24 movable vertebrae which are designed to bend and flex in six different directions while still retaining their support role.

If two vertebrae become stuck (fixated) in one section of the spine, two other vertebrae somewhere in the spine will begin to move more, to compensate for the fixated section. This can mean for example, that the top of your spine underneath the skull, can feel pressure and pain, because it is adapting to two vertebrae lower down in the neck that are fixated which you don't feel at all.

Depending on the type of stress your body is under, and the amount of falls, accidents, and traumas you may have experienced, you may have a wild mish-mash of fixation/compensation problems in the spine that only a skilled practitioner of Articular Therapy would be qualified to address.

57. What Is Another Function of the Spine that is Crucial to Health?

Another aspect of the skeleton, more specifically the spinal vertebra, is that they house and protect the nerves regulating bodily functions as they exit the spine.

The nervous system, including the brain, spinal cord, and peripheral nerves, control and coordinate every single function in the cells of the body. The skeleton's "hard" protection of the "soft" nervous system mandates that problems with its mechanical function can create neurological disturbances elsewhere.

This includes the type of symptoms you can feel, such as joint pain, pain radiating down the arm or leg, a sore hip, etc. But it also includes nerve function symptoms you can't feel such as internal organ problems and immune system disorders, which involve the autonomic nerves that don't carry pain fibers.

Because the nerves must exit between the vertebras to get to their ultimate destination, there is a chance that a difficult fall or car accident can cause the vertebras to slide out of their normal movement patterns, and actually impinge or put pressure on a nerve as it exits the spine. Chiropractors have treated this problem for years as a "pinched" nerve.

Few people know that the first Chiropractic patient was "cured" of deafness, and the second of heart disease. Chiropractors don't "treat your spine." They remove pressure on the nerves caused by the vertebra, and this allows the body to then heal itself. Denial of the obvious realities of this connection by the medical "profession" still blows my mind.

58. How Does A "Pinched Nerve" create Neurological Dysfunction?

There are two mechanisms by which a "pinched nerve" can cause problems. The first is that you have the "hard" bone pressing on the "soft" nerve.

This disturbs the flow of energy going through the nerve; in the same way that stepping on a hose would block water flowing to a garden plant. If you step on a hose while watering your flowers, what effect would that have on the flowers?

Another less well-known factor is that a fixation on one side of a vertebra can cause the other side to *stretch* the nerve (through hyper-mobility as discussed earlier.) The "stretching" of the nerve sheath as it exits the spine causes "too much" energy to flow along the nerve. This in turn causes the glands and organs to speed up out of time with need.

As both Chiropractors and Acupuncturists have said, "too much" or "too little" energy can cause disease. When the flow of nerve energy is mechanically altered at the spine, whichever way it goes "too much" or "too little," this creates a plethora of problems that are unrecognizable to the untrained medical practitioner (as well as "the lied to" public) as being related to their original cause.

59. What is a Specific Example of Spinal Fixations Causing "Unusual" Body Symptoms In Other Areas?

Because nerves control and coordinate all parts of the human body, this means spinal nerve pressure can cause malfunctions in any organ and/or body part due to its importance in protecting the nerves. Let's take the bladder as one example.

The bladder is basically a muscular sac that holds liquid waste in the body until it fills up enough for the bladder to signal the brain that it's time to go to the bathroom. The muscles of the bladder are under nerve control as well as the nerves signaling the status of the bladder to the brain. The ability to "hold" or "let loose" of muscular function occurs because of a signal from the nerves.

If the nerve connected to the bladder is not in 100% communication with the brain, that means the brain might not even know the bladder is full, and thus lets the bladder release while a person is asleep. Known as enuresis, or bed-wetting, this condition is often cured when a person goes to a chiropractor and gets adjustments of the vertebra that house the nerve going to the bladder.

This is one of many examples, where the urologist, who most people would consider to be the "bladder specialist", would have no treatment therapy that works. Yet a chiropractor, who might be treating the patient for lower back pain, (which would be consistent with misaligned vertebra going to the bladder) can get a positive result even though the patient may never have even told the chiropractor about the bed-wetting in the first place.

60. What Is Another Example Of Spinal Fixations Causing "Unusual" Body Problems In Other Areas?

There is a famous advertisement used in the Chiropractic Profession that goes something like this:

Chiropractor Gets Patient Pregnant!

It attracts the reader to read the salacious details of the story of the Chiropractor (often enough a female) going to jail for "getting the patient" pregnant. But as it turns out; the patient was a long-suffering woman who had been attempting for years to get pregnant by any means necessary.

As a result of the Chiropractor (male or female) restoring the neurological function of the woman's body, presumably the nerves going to the uterus or ovaries, the woman was able to achieve a natural pregnancy to term without complications.

Not only is this a regular occurrence in Chiropractors offices, it is also true for many patients who were able to get pregnant but were continually losing their pregnancy in the early months without any medical explanation.

61. What is Yet Another Example of Spinal Fixations Causing "Unusual" Body Problems In Other Areas?

There is symptom called "phantom limb" syndrome. This is the perception of pain or sensations in a limb that has been amputated. Sometimes the amputation was somebody's brilliant idea to treat the pain in the first place.

Patients with this condition experience their limb as if it were still attached to their body as the brain continues to receive messages from nerves that originally carried impulses from the missing limb.

It's very clear to me that this problem is due to the person still having a spine, and whatever the original injury was that caused either the loss of the limb, or the reason for the amputation, was traumatic enough to have caused the original spinal fixation in the first place. The idea that this problem is often described as "psychological" defies belief.

Chiropractic treatment to remove the fixation, or "subluxation" as it's often called, would correct this problem.

More to the point is that many people have "phantom limb" pain *while they still have their limb.*

Their pain is originating due to their spinal fixation. Because they still have their limb, they get thousands of dollars of physical therapy or whatever useless therapy you like where the pain hurts, yet the cause, coming from a spinal fixation, is never addressed.

Chapter Six:

What Is Deeper Look at the Digestive System?

62. What is the Importance of the Digestive System In GHS?

In order for the cells of your body to receive the nutrients and vital materials they need, you have to drink liquids and eat food.

Your digestive tract oversees this miracle of transformation. It takes the food you eat, which is outside your body, and breaks it down mechanically and chemically into a form of nutrition that can be released in the blood and accepted by the cells.

If any part of the digestive tract becomes overloaded or diseased, then symptoms will develop. If they are not monitored and taken care of, these symptoms will progress into full-blown disease processes.

We all have to eat; yet it's the rare person who has a digestive system that has not been abused.

This is because the western lifestyle has created damage to the digestive systems of humans over time due to the manufacturing and promoting of unhealthful foods.

Although we know much more about nutrition and digestive function than we did 200 years ago, the dietary changes that have become commonplace in today's world have done long-term damage to the health of the individual and society.

We are now much more susceptible to early diseases due to chronic dietary abuse, which is often long-term and difficult to reverse.

63. Which is More Important: A Good Diet, or a Good Digestive System?

If you eat a "perfect diet" (whatever that is), with a bad digestive system, guess what? Your body won't absorb and assimilate your perfect nutritional diet no matter how much it costs.

If you eat a crappy diet, and we all know what that is, with a strong and dynamic digestive system, guess what? Your body will take and absorb the maximum nutritional value from the garbage you eat and you could appear to be healthy to all concerned.

Obviously, I'm not recommended that eating a lousy diet is a good idea. But I do want to emphasize this point that having a strong and effective digestive system and HOW you eat is more crucial for sustaining and maintaining health than WHAT you eat.

Healthy digestive organs start with having a strong and unobstructed nerve supply. Next you have to pay attention to what you eat, eating in a manner that is comfortable for YOUR body. Finally, you have to make sure that you are NOT poisoning yourself by what you eat and drink, and that's not easy in today's world.

64. What Are The Important Organs of Digestion?

The important organs of digestion are your:

- Eyes and Nose
- Mouth and Chewing
- Stomach
- Pancreas
- Gall Bladder
- Small Intestine
- Ileocecal Valve
- Large Intestine

If any of these areas of digestive function interest you, I have written a complete book on this topic with unusual details and insights about digestive problems and the mysterious types of symptoms they can cause. It is called:

The Digestive Awareness Diet: You Are HOW You Eat

And can be easily ordered through Amazon.com.

Chapter Seven:

What Is Deeper Look at the Hormonal System?

65. What Does the Hormonal System Do?

The hormonal system is the watchdog of internal chemistry controlling and regulating many of the body's important internal cellular functions.

In conjunction with the master controller the nerve system, the hormonal system monitors a range of bodily processes and reacts on a second-by-second basis to maintain a balance in the body called homeostasis.

If homeostasis goes "out of bounds" then it's the hormonal system's job to reinstate homeostasis to the best of its ability.

When there have been long-term internal or external stressors on the body, then the function of the hormonal system degrades over time, creating problems that accelerate chronic disease and death to the body.

By assessing and locating these problem areas in the hormonal glands, GHS can often reverse what many medical experts refer to as "incurable conditions."

The premise of Generic Human Studies is that when the spine (including the skeleton), the digestive system, and the hormonal system are all working in harmony, then the body already knows how to take care of itself.

The goal of GHS is for each individual to seek information and monitor themselves with these systems in mind, to correct and maintain wellness.

66. What Are The Important Organs of the Hormonal System?

The important organs of hormonal regulation are your:

- Pituitary
- Thyroid
- Pancreas
- Adrenal
- Orchic Glands (the testes and the ovaries)

67. What Is the Function of the Pituitary?

The pituitary gland is often called the "master" gland of the endocrine system, because it controls the functions of the other endocrine glands. It secretes several hormones and monitors their release to the blood in conjunction with the hypothalamus.

The pituitary gland is about the size of a pea and is located at the base of the brain. This gland is attached to the hypothalamus (a part of the brain that influences the pituitary gland) by nerve fibers.

68. WHAT IS THE FUNCTION OF THE THYROID?

The thyroid gland manufactures thyroid hormone, which is a key aspect to the regulatory function of the hormonal system.

It is located in the middle of the lower neck, below the larynx (voice box) and just above your collarbones. Shaped like a "bow tie," it has two halves (lobes): a right lobe and a left lobe.

It regulates homeostasis, internal heat and cold regulation, energy levels, and many other important bodily functions.

69. What Is the Function of the Adrenals?

The Adrenal; glands produce hormones that you can't live without, such as the sex hormones and cortisol, which is released in response to stress and has many other functions.

Your adrenal glands are located near the top of each kidney. They also produce hormones to regulate fluid and salt balance in the body.

70. What Is the Function of the Orchic Glands?

The orchic glands are another name for the testes and the ovaries, also called gonads. They are the male and female equivalents that create and release the sex hormones in the body. Testosterone is produced by the testes, and Estrogen, is produced by the ovaries.

The sex hormones have a huge impact in various human abilities and behaviors, of which scientifically we don't know a lot, even today. Simply giving a person the identical dose of a hormone does not create the same effect in similar individuals.

There is a lot more we need to know about all the hormonal functions.

71. How Does a Malfunctioning Hormonal System Create Health Problems?

To make a long story short, if your hormonal glands become depleted, this will have a detrimental effect on every aspect of your body, mind, and relationships. If your hormonal glands can be supported and nutritionally balanced, this will make a dramatic difference in your health.

As a natural health practitioner with over 30 years experience I've have used natural nutritional/hormonal therapies which, when indicated, have made all the difference for my depressed and compromised immune patients.

72. How Can An Individual Reading This Book learn Enough to Diagnose and Treat Hormonal Problems?

Two points I would like to make here. The hormonal glands are the last defense against disease. If they go, you are gone already.

Spinal care and Digestive care are the key methods for keeping hormonal problems at bay, and both are readily available for the most part.

I regret that this topic is where the generic nature of my knowledge does indeed become too technical, and I can't give you a general enough set of guidelines to enable a person to self-treat or diagnose a hormonal problem as I have with my other body, mind, and relationship insights.

In some countries my completely natural methods have been outlawed by the powers that be, and in truth, if you do have a hormonally involved condition you need to be monitored and treated by someone who knows what they are doing.

If you've gotten this far and think that hormonal issues might be part of your quest, I'd be happy to help you if possible, based on your situation, country, and other factors.

In the last ten years, there has been a sharp increase in the monitoring and treating of hormonal problems using sophisticated, yet easily accessible, lab tests which is finally working its way into public awareness.

73. How Does GHS Help You With Your Worst Body Problem?

These guidelines are presented to give the USER valuable clues to understanding complex health problems and conditions.

What is the CAUSE of your worst body problem?

Is it a specific articular joint pain, a digestive organ malfunction, or a hidden hormonal imbalance?

Chapter Eight:

What Is GHS Mind Work?

74. WHAT IS THE GENERIC HUMAN MIND?

Hardware by itself has no practical function. The human brain and nervous system (as hardware) are similar to a computer in that neither will function without a software operating system.

The neurological hardware of the brain consists of the Left Brain and the Right Brain. Think of the mind as the software package that allows these two brains to connect and communicate with each other.

The most important thing to know about "the mind" is that it represents the operating system of the human bio-computer.

75. What are the Three Parts of the Generic Human Mind?

For the purpose of clarity and to discuss the function of each part of the mind, GHS calls the three parts of the mind:

- The "Inner Parent" Mind (Mental/Thoughts)
- The "Inner Child" Mind (Emotional/Feelings)
- The "Higher Self" Mind (Spiritual/Social)

Each person's "mind" consists of these three separate aspects, which are given different names so they can be discussed in relation to their differing functionality.

Your day-to-day experience of "mind" is in reality an exchange of communication between your three component minds about what to do next in your life and why.

From these interactions between the three "minds" spring all other forms of mental computations.

76. What is the "Inner Parent" Mind?

The "Inner Parent" mind is what most people typically call the personality or "ego." It is the rational thinking part of our mind that makes decisions based on facts, and logic. It is highly developed in rational thinking and intellectual activity. It enjoys drawing up boundaries, legal documents, and using facts and figures.

It is the mind that is in play when you are trying to be polite and formal. Acting as the conscious mind, it is involved in the day-to-day planning and strategizing of your life. Although it has some power and control because it is the "conscious mind," it's not the only part of your mind with an opinion. It is completely distinct and separate from the "Inner Child" Mind.

77. What Creates the "Inner Parent" Mind?

The "Inner Parent" mind is created from the style of parenting you received as a child. When a child is young, he/she copies and mimics exactly the most important source of his/her survival, the adult parents. Whatever type of parenting is used on a child, he or she will adapt and mold this into his/her "inner parent" mind.

Your Inner Parent is biologically programmed with the style and formatting of your outer parenting as a child. If you have Chinese parents, you learned to speak Chinese. If you have French parents, you speak French.

But more importantly, even the subtle and nuanced aspects of your outer parenting are part of your own Inner Parent. Before you ever became aware of it, your "Inner Parent" mind learned to copy exactly and react identically to the parenting you received as a child. You retain this early programming even though now you are an adult.

As you grow during childhood your family, schooling, and social environment all contribute to your Inner Parent.

When a person reaches "adulthood" they continue to study, work, and socialize in society and gain an even deeper and more rounded aspect to their "Inner Parent" mind, thus becoming a mature member of society.

78. WHAT IS THE "INNER CHILD" MIND?

The "Inner Child" Mind is often called the unconscious mind, but it doesn't have to be unconscious.

This mind is where the emotions and feelings operate. It is also the holistic mind, dealing with patterns and systems. This mind is concerned with the here and now, especially if it involves feeling comfortable or pleasure. It is the mind that expresses curiosity and wonder.

This mind is also in charge of stored emotions, and is where all the memories are kept. All the genuine emotions originate from the "Inner Child" mind. It is also the mental software aspect most in touch with the hardware of the five senses.

79. How Does the "Inner Parent" programming Affect Adulthood?

If you had a positive set of outer parents, who loved, supported, and nurtured you in a positive manner, then your Inner Parent could be very happy as an adult just enjoying life and wondering why so many other people were having problems all the time.

If you had a negative set of outer parents or parental upbringing, you could be sad, anxious, and unhappy as an adult along with a variety of other coping mental issues, even though your life was relatively comfortable and secure. You might never recognize the source of your angst as unfortunate parenting that was programmed before you had a chance to become aware of it.

80. What Creates the "Inner Child" Mind?

The "Inner Child" mind is who you were as a child, even though you may now be an adult. It is the emotional, enthusiastic part of your mind you were born with, unless it has been thwarted and abused during your upbringing.

As a child this is your most dominant viewpoint. Your Inner Child also matures through various stages as your brain and nerve system grows and matures during childhood.

As a child matures, he or she is taught and acclimated to his or her cultural environment. This voice remains strong in terms of its personality; however the voice of the Inner Child could also be suppressed or denied. A child's parents, teachers, employers, political systems, etc., could do this. (or not) There is a wide variety of potential programming that can occur in the human experience.

81. What Creates the "Inner Conversations" of the Mind?

If you could attach electrodes to your brain and this could print out what you are thinking, you would find this stream of consciousness called "thinking" by most people would actually take place in the form of a conversation.

One side of your mind, the "Inner Parent" would be recognized as "parenting" while the other side of the conversation, the "Inner Child" would be responding back, just like a child. By reading and evaluating this "print-out" you would be able to tell whether the internal parenting was essentially positive or negative.

This conversation would read identically to any recorded outer parents conversations interacting with his/her outer child during the day.

82. What Form Do Your "Inner Conversations" take In Conversation?

Basically, within your "inner conversations," you are "parenting yourself" and "being parented" inside your mind. And this is happening throughout your life, at every age.

This occurs whether you were brought up in Tibet, Iceland, Jamaica, L.A., Amsterdam, Singapore, Perth, India, China; need I go on? All of humanity, every single person without damaged hardware, is self-parenting, has always been, and will always be self-parenting.

Whether they like it, know about it, or care, they have no other software option. Whatever language he/she speaks, doesn't matter. If you say it's not true, then this is the result of a Self-parenting decision you chose to make that claim.

These "Inner Conversations" are the two main parts of your mind, communicating with each other non-stop throughout the day. They are the filter through which you make every decision (large or small) in your life.

They are estimated to flow at a rate of between 800-1200 words a minute.

83. How is Brain Research Related to the "Inner Conversations" of the Mind?

The brain, which reflects the "hardware" of the mind, has an interesting two-sided lobe arrangement typically called the Left Brain and Right Brain. There has been much research on the functioning of these two sides of the brain from the 1950s on. There is much we know about the function of these two brains, and yet so much more we don't.

In practical terms, and for the purpose of discussion, the Left Brain is the hardware for the "Inner Parent" mind, and the Right Brain is the hardware for the "Inner Child" mind.

These two minds communicate to each other and are only connected to each other through a pencil-sized bundle of nerves called the corpus callosum. (The early research on brain function began when a brain surgeon decided that cutting this bundle of nerve bundles between the two brains would be a good idea.)

If you were to study and analyze how the two brains function, you would see that the Left Brain acts much like an outer parent communicating with an outer child.

The Right Brain would be responding and originating thougts in a similar manner to the way an outer child thinks and communicates with an outer parent.

84. What is the "Operating System" of the Human Bio-Computer?

This operating system of the human bio-computer, called the mind by most people, functions through a process best described as "Self-Parenting."

The style of parenting you received as a child created this "programming", which is installed neurologically from outside the hardware itself. There are genuine and scientifically verified cases of children who have been brought up by wolves, and guess what? Their software behaved and acted exactly like wolves.

The Inner Conversations you have in your mind are the Left-Brain talking to the Right-Brain (and vice versa) in the same manner that your Outer Parents interacted with you when you were an Outer Child (and vice versa).

Everything you do in your outer life stems from decisions you make using this operating system. That is why I call the mind the "operating system of the human bio-computer."

85. How Does Self-Parenting Apply to the Student of GHS?

A person may be totally unaware of his/her own personal version of "operating system" going on inside his/her mind, but they will be acting from these sets of instructions whether they realize this or not.

Students of GHS consciously study their Inner Conversations so they can learn to become a more positive Inner Parent to their Inner Child. It's very much like when outer parents take an outer parenting class to become better parents. They do this by practicing a half-hour of conscious self-parenting to start their day.

Practicing conscious Self-Parenting is like sending your Inner Parent to parenting school. You can learn which parts of your Inner Parent have learned the wrong lessons, and "re-learn" them in a more positive manner. After some experience and practical principles, a person can see/hear/feel the deeper patterns, and if negative, work to change them in conjunction with the support of their Inner Child.

Typically, the Inner Child becomes very excited when its Inner Parent finally comes around to doing something about the unconscious/dysfunctional parenting that you inherited without edits from your outer parenting.

86. Are There Any Bad Consequences to the Practice of Self-Parenting As Might Apply to the Student of GHS?

I have observed a specific and observable phenomenon of the Self-Parenting process that I feel honor-bound to communicate with the potential student of GHS.

The Inner Child doesn't like it when the Inner Parent starts Self-parenting—does it for a few weeks, and then stops once the Inner Parent feels better.

Some people start Self-parenting, for reasons that might not be that conscious. Maybe they've had a break-up, or their friend made them, or they really were just goofing around. I don't mind if they stop, it's their life and there's no rule that a person has to be consciously self-parenting.

But for the Inner Child, this is perhaps the very first time he/she has ever been heard, at least partially, in their whole life. This would be the equivalent of the Inner Child having grown up in prison all its life. Then one day out of the blue getting to go to Disneyland for a half-hour a day for a short period of time; and then not, again, ever.

Inner Child says,

"Ouch!"

87. So What Are The Bad consequences That Might Apply to the Student of GHS?

So just for the record, I want to make this point. This doesn't apply if you were not really trying to practice Self-Parenting, but it does if you gave it some serious effort and experienced some of the magic that positive Self-Parenting brings to the new practitioner.

As an Inner Parent you pretty much only have one second chance to begin again, and this time please keep it going if you do make it.

What happens is a bit contradictory but hear me out. The Inner Child was upset when you quit listening to it for 30 minutes a day. Especially if the Inner Parent used the energy to solve some problem on the Inner Parents mind and didn't even throw the Inner Child a bone.

If you are a true student of GHS, you want to be practicing conscious Self-parenting. That's a given. If you did do S/P once before in the past, but then stopped for some reason. Beware that when you restart for a second time, the Inner Child will often intentionally throw obstacles in your path. You will certainly be susceptible to some tongue-lashing or resistance for a period of time.

88. What Would Be Some consequences If You Started and Stopped S/P for a Third Time As A Student of GHS?

If you, as the Inner Parent, attempt to start Self-parenting again for a third time, your Inner Child will make you wish you were never born. Or it simply won't buy it. You won't get a peep the whole 30 minutes. It will just shut down and stubbornly refuse to participate. All to test you and make you quit, so it won't be hurt again.

I'm hoping this sheds light on this process. You need to know that if you want to start this process again to be prepared. It will take some hard work and assistance for your Inner Parent to hold on to become Intermediate in the process.

89. If Self-Parenting Is So Good, Why Does the Inner Parent Stop the Practice?

I've observed 2 distinct sets of Inner Parents in Self-Parenting. One is the strong negative IP and the other is the weak negative IP. The good thing about a strong negative IP, is that even though they are probably strongly abusing their IC, once they commit to the process, they go for it in a big way.

The strong IP uses its strength to follow the rules exactly. It does everything by the book. They never miss a session. If they make some of the classic mistakes and feel the negative result, they find out what they were doing wrong by asking me or rereading the book or module.

The weak negative IP is a very different situation.

90. What Is the Trouble with the Weak Inner Parent?

The weak Inner Parent has a very unfortunate predicament. It doesn't take a stand. It doesn't follow through. It begins things but doesn't finish. It gets a fabulous response from the IC and then forgets about it 3 hours later. It doesn't have the drive or determination it takes to succeed with the process, much less get to Intermediate Status.

I often find the weak IP has a smart and determined IC, who tries to drive the process, but even this is not ideal. The best thing the IP can do is try to find a support group, but that's next to impossible at the moment. I can't even find a support group.

This is the IP for who the IC says clearly, over and over, do this, and do that, nagging if you will. Yet, the IP doesn't make a move. I've read sessions from the weak IP's session book, and there were weeks, sometimes months of the same plea, over and over. The advice was exactly and perfectly what was needed in the situation. Still, a vague shrug and "I don't know why I can't do it?"

Even I don't know what to do about the weak IP. The obvious idea is to go over to their side of the seesaw (see next section) and make them do what they are clearly supposed to do. However, I don't. If that person consults with me, I feel obligated to hammer them a bit. I do support the IC as much as I can, but it's not pretty.

91. So What Are Other Aspects of Self-parenting that Might Apply to the Student of GHS?

Self-Parenting, whether you do it consciously or not, is of no never-mind to me; it's your decision, on your own seesaw as we might say in GHR.

In this vein as an observer of this process, I have a story to tell. One of my early students was practicing Self-parenting during a month course and had related some amazing stories. All of our class was pretty astounded by her experiences.

I happened to see her a few weeks after the class, so I asked her how her self-parenting was going. "Oh yeah, self-parenting; I had to stop that." was her reply. I was incredulous but I did ask her why. Her answer, "I found out I couldn't lie to my Inner Child anymore." So, she stopped her conscious S/P as a strategy of her Inner Parent to "win" over her Inner Child and not have to keep justifying her lies all the time. Her choice!

Another story I like from the early days was during an intro meeting. One of the "sharers" told his story about how much work he'd done and how committed he was to self-parenting. But, then he ended his perfect speech with, "Now that I've found out about that litter sucker. I'm going to whip him into shape." while smashing his fist into his palm. We didn't see him at the second session.

So for the general public, it's your decision. I don't mind either way. For the GHS Student, it's mandatory unless you are doing it perfectly already and that's hard to prove. But even then, it's up to you. It won't get done any other way.

92. Why Does One's Self-Parenting Style Concern the Student of GHS?

A person's self-parenting style can be positive or negative. Typically there is more negative than positive. Or certainly, it is the negative aspects of your self-parenting style that are giving you grief.

To become aware of your own specific pattern of Self-parenting, special techniques and methods are needed to slow down and evaluate your inner conversations. These are described and presented in the book, *SELF-PARENTING: The Complete Guide to Your Inner Conversations.*

The GHS student would use this system to learn what kind of Self-Parenting Style he or she has and is currently operating under.

In other words, what is your Self-Parenting Style? How do you, as the Inner Parent, parent your Inner Child inside your mind?

93. How Can a Person's Self-Parenting Style Be Assessed?

Self-Parenting can be assessed as being mostly positive, mostly negative, or somewhere in-between.

If you had a positive set of outer parents, who loved, supported, and nurtured you in a positive manner, then you will automatically have a positive Self-Parenting Style.

If your parents were mostly abusive, or neglected you, then you will have been given a negative or abusive Self-Parenting Style.

Most people find themselves with a mixture of positive and negative Self-Parenting.

Each human is operating their mind according to the way they were brought up, combined with what they have learned on their own.

For the committed practitioner of Self-Parenting, as measured by being of Intermediate status, even the worst Self-parenting style can be corrected and reversed with help. Not that it's easy, but clear and steady progress makes it attainable.

94. What Is the GHS Student's First Goal as a Self-Parenting Practitioner

If you wanted a real test of Self-Parenting and how it would be in your life if you did it, you'd need to at least aim for the Intermediate Status as a Practitioner.

This is approximately a 3-6 month, on average, process. It involves 10 Steps which aren't that hard, but are each required. The steps to Self-Parenting are outlined to be as simple as can be. That doesn't mean it's easy.

I describe the 10 Steps to Intermediate Practice as 10 large boulders in a raging river. The boulders are big, they are high and dry. They are close together and can be easily traversed if you don't get side-tracked.

If you stay on the boulders, do one at a time, you'll get across no problems. If you dawdle, or miss a boulder, or decide to go swimming, you'll be so far down the river so fast, you'll never even know you're not practicing anymore.

These 10 steps are there to help the GHS Student. I've met people who have practiced conscious Self-parenting on their own for two years or more, who weren't as "far" with their personal process as a 3-6 month Intermediate Practitioner.

However, once they did learn about the boulders to cross the river, they progressed very quickly because staying with Self-parenting, for that long even at a lesser level, is pretty impressive right there. No Inner Child would give up on an Inner Parent who did that.

95. What Is An Interesting Phenomena Concerning the Blue Book?

This might not be the place for this, but I'd like to say it anyway in case there is a GHS Student for whom this might apply.

What we call the "Blue Book", *The Self-Parenting Program: Core Guidelines for the Self-Parenting Practitioner,* is out there available to anyone. However, if you read it before practicing Self-Parenting for at least 6 months to a year, and that's doing everything right, you won't even have a clue what I'm saying in there.

It's easy enough to read, it's in English. But the reality for the unconscious reader is not the same as for an experienced practitioner. For those practitioners who were practicing "perfectly" and did read it at 6 months, 1 year, even 5 years later, they always find that I totally rewrote it since the last time they read it.

If it's the first book that you've read about Self-Parenting, my apologies, as it's pretty useless as an introduction. The only negative comment yet about the books on Amazon, came from such a reader of the Blue Book in the UK, who got a quick response back from one of our practitioners. Sorry, that's just the way it is.

If you have been practicing S/P and you haven't read the Blue Book, for a while. I advise reading it again. Just to make sure. The "Yellow Book" is best book to introduce the practice. Then get to the website for the "23 Tips" and the "10 Steps."

96. WHAT IS ONE LAST THING MY INNER CHILD WANTS ME TO SAY ABOUT SELF-PARENTING?

Self-Parenting is "Inner Parent" work, not "Inner Child" work. Any Inner Child will respond willingly to sincere Self-parenting by its Inner Parent. This is a given. Its part of what you get if the Inner Parent starts the practice.

If the Inner Parent doesn't want to, or try, or is weak, or has negative traits, or is too busy, or doesn't have time, or will do it when they get the chance, or tried it and it didn't work, and all other forms of IP bs excuses; all that is on the Inner Parent's side of the Self-Parenting Seesaw.

Playing la-dee-dah balloons and birthdays with your Inner Child is not Self-Parenting. That's "Inner Child" work, it is okay. It's got a place as a therapy if you choose it, but it's not what Self-Parenting is about. Self-Parenting is so far beyond that crap, you have no idea.

Self-Parenting is about consciously parenting your own Inner Child, as an Inner Parent, inside your mind. Without that equation, it's not what I get every day still from my Inner Parent.

97. What is the "High Self" Mind?

The High Self mind represents the elements or aspects of thinking most people consider "spiritual."

This third element of mental functioning is the connection each individual feels with a personal God, a Spiritual Source, or a Higher Power. It could be considered the "soul" or spirit mind that exists before birth and after death. There are many names for the universal aspect of this part of the human mind.

This self is not "outside" the person, but within. It typically functions as a tiny voice, which provides insight, direction, and motivation to those lucky enough to hear it.

All people have the ability to communicate with their "High Self" Mind but the average human does not recognize this part of their three-part mind.

For those individuals who do become aware of this aspect of the mind, they describe a remarkably similar experience regardless of their culture, religion, or political social system.

98. What is An Interesting Possibility Considering the "High Self" Mind?

I do believe that there are a fair number of people who hear their higher self mind so often and so strongly that it's not really a big deal. Even to the point of it being his/her dominant inner voice. They might not even know that other people aren't doing this because they just assume everybody is like them. They are usually the ones helping everybody.

They could also be the ones following any recognized religion, who, since they already have a strong connection to their High Self, intuitively see/hear/feel the truth of their religious path, and just follow it because it's the one they were born into.

If you'd like to read the biography of a "natural" high self driven person, I suggest checking out the story of the "Peace Pilgrim" who was clearly as enlightened as one can be. Her story is as real in western terms, as any Vedantic pilgrim's story, and yet even more incredible for the time, place, and manner in which she achieved her ascendancy.

99. How Does the "High Self" Mind Enter Into the Picture As Far as Self-Parenting Is Concerned?

Connecting to the "High Self" mind is something the Inner Parent and Inner Child minds can do when they get together and decide to communicate with and listen to the "High Self" mind. I believe Max Freedom Long's Huna books describe this process as clearly as can be. What he says, I believe.

The "High Self" can also directly communicate to the two lower selves when it sees fit.

I have seen more than a handful of Self-Parenting practitioners start Self-Parenting and within a few months be closely attuned to their High Self mind.

100. How Important Is THE "High Self" Mind in Generic Human Studies?

Not that important. It's nice if you can get it but it doesn't really matter. The High Self is the High Self, by definition it is perfect beyond any human's ability to comprehend, regardless of which religion you follow. All the founders' of all the religions said the same thing, "It is perfection and words cannot describe!"

So, each person's Higher Self is doing for him/her exactly what is perfect for that individual, and we have no say about that other person's status either way with his/her High Self.

101. What's Another Problem with the "High Self" Mind from the GHS POV?

GHS is only about three dimensions. It's the ones we all can see and feel. This is a physics and math thing, but if you read (or know) Flatland, by Edwin A Abbot, you will know what I'm talking about.

I believe as residents on this planet earth we are limited to three dimensions, and this is all we can third-party verify as being "real" ala the way science is agreed upon to be "real." So when talking GHS we stay within a third-party verifiable system.

However, there is mathematical proof of 4th, and 5th dimensions, as well as science fiction speaking to this topic for years. The 4th dimension is not available to us in three dimensions. And if we could travel to it as in Flatland, we would be able to see this (spiritual dimension stuff) as our insides.

That's where the High Self is, God, whatever you call God, no God if you like, whatever you say it is for you God. So for what it's worth, that's my personal theory on the High Self concept. I like it myself, but I've only got my own opinion.

In the three-dimensional world, I can prove everything GHS has to say. However, it's more up to you to "get" GHS, rather than for me to ram it down your throat, and this might be the only place I ever try.

102. Why Are "Spiritual" Topics and Issues NOT Part of Generic Human Studies?

Technically speaking, the "High Self" Mind is in the category of "spiritual" discussion. Spiritual awareness and reality are specifically personal and are beyond any other human's right or ability to diagnose or control.

Not that this stops people from trying. There are many "religions" and "philosophical systems" that profess "spiritual" awareness. From the GHS perspective; these groups are seen as social organizations, man-made, that exist for social reasons which fulfill a deep human need and are legitimate for this purpose.

In Generic Human Studies, when someone tries to control or comment on another person's "spirituality," he/she is by definition incorrect. Another person has no way of truly knowing what is spiritual or not for another person. He/she can only comment on his/her own awareness for his/her own High Self. Spiritual is already perfect and indescribable; what's to talk about?

103. How Does Generic Human Studies Approach "spiritual" Topics?

Generic Human Studies as defined involves every aspect concerning the human experience up to and excluding spirituality.

Spirituality, the existence or non-existence of a god and similar topics are simply not part of the body of work of Generic Human Studies. Each person's own spiritual opinion for him/her self is as valid as any other persons.

Much of the early efforts of learning Generic Human Studies go toward distinguishing the personal elements of body, mind, and relations from "spiritual subjects" and God's existence for the USER.

The reason for this is when a body, mind, or relational problem bothers people long enough with no clear source or solution, one's only hope left is to pray or pay for a "spiritual healing."

With GHS, many of these "spiritual problems" become easily resolved as they were never spiritual problems in the first place. They were something gone wrong with the body, mind, and/or a relation.

104. What Kinds of Causes For Human Problems is Generic Human Studies Looking For?

If something is spiritually caused, it's outside of our control. It's from a source we can't quantify. If something "bad" happens here in the three-dimensions that is completely 100% spiritual, this doesn't make it hurt any less.

In Generic Human Studies we look for the causes of human problems stemming from the physical, emotional, or mental functions within your body and/or mind, and/or relations in which you are involved.

We know from experience, if we fix those, many of your "spiritual problems" will be magically solved as you will begin working things out for yourself.

105. What is the GHS Way to Sort Out "Spiritual" Problems from "Real World" problems?

One way to sort this out, in case you aren't quite with me yet, is to (if you are currently seeking a spiritual solution to a problem in your life) ask yourself the following question:

"If my spiritual problems were solved,
how would my life be different?"

If your answer involves people, places, money, or anything to do with your body, mind, or a relation, then your problem is a human problem, not a spiritual one.

And if it doesn't, then you do undoubtedly do need a spiritual solution which unfortunately, GHS does not have.

106. What is Your Worst Mind Problem?

Are you happy most of the time? Do you feel fulfilled with most of your activities during your day?

If not, then quite possibly you are experiencing a mind problem that originates from the style of parenting you received as a child.

Even though you may now be an adult, your pattern of self-parenting is deeply internal to the functioning of your current conscious mind. It can take many weeks/months to dig deeply into your pattern of inner conversation to see where the true problems lie.

If this is an area of further interest to you, search Amazon for a copy of *SELF-PARENTING: The Complete Guide to Your Inner Conversations.*

I recommend you purchase the new (not used) versions as many subtle changes were made to correct earlier versions.

This technology was the first Generic Human Studies information to become publicly available and there is a wide body of knowledge about this subject in the Self-Parenting books and modules on the www.selfparenting.com website.

Chapter Nine:

What Is GHS Relations Work?

107. What is a Generic Human Relation?

A Generic Human Relation is what I call the mechanism by which two individual humans link to each other to fulfill personal and mutual needs.

A human being has many needs and he or she does not get them met by working alone. Let's face it. If we were the only person on earth we wouldn't last long.

In fact, human society is the collection of individuals working together to create and meet the needs and goals of human living.

108. How is a "Generic Human Relation" Different From "Regular" Human Relations?

All human societies have similar roles to their relations. This includes all the societies who have ever dwelled. What Generic Human Studies does is establish an ideal sample model, one for each of the main relations that all cultures have.

This would be 12 "generic" human relations.

What Generic Human Studies presents is an outline of the 12 categories of relations entered into by two individuals, as one-on-one experiences within human society, distilled to their very essence to explain and explore how they operate.

Generic Human Relations (GHR) is the system of understanding the anatomy and physiology of how relations work as well as a system for evaluating the success or failure of a relation.

Each of the 12 generic relations has a generic model that can be outlined and studied.

Studying the 12 generic relational models helps GHR students determine when they are in a relation, out of a relation, and/or a myriad of other aspects concerning relations. GHR has an extensive and ever growing body of knowledge concerning human relations.

109. What are the Three Main Types of Human Relations?

The study of GHR begins with the three main types of personal human relations. They are:

- Family
- Social
- Work

Each relational type contains the personal relations needed to meet those types of needs for individuals in their particular human society.

110. What About All the Other Kinds of Human Relations?

The study of group dynamics, corporations, politics, and interactions between groups of groups of people is outside the subject area of generic human studies. Also, anything possible that *could* occur between two people is not our concern.

There is a fourth type of one-on-one human relation, loosely called Professional. These are the relations that typically involve teaching, learning, healing, among others and are provided through the governance of society as a function for the benefit of its members.

Professional relations typically involve the exchange of money for services rendered, which is by definition "professional," and are not included with the main three types of generic "personal" relations. Each human has/needs personal relationships. Professional relationships technically are optional.

111. WHAT ARE THE "PERSONAL" TYPES OF RELATIONS?

In GHR, we are concerned with the individual human in his/her "generic" form.

In your personal life, as the USER of GHR, the relations that are considered "personal" are those that involve *you* with one other person in a specific interaction based on meeting each other's "personal" needs.

A personal relation means that it is:

- YOUR Family relations
- YOUR Social relations
- YOUR Work relations

It's the human interactions you are personally experiencing.

Your personal family relations may be vastly different from their generic equivalent. Your social and work relations may also be highly individualized and unique.

Each of your personal Family, Social, and Work relations are evaluated as single entities through comparison with its generic equivalent.

The closer your "personal" relations match their generic equivalents, the happier you would be expected to be. The more your "personal" relation differs from its generic equivalent, the more it explains your current problems with that relation.

112. What About Relations When They Involve More Than One Person?

Many more human relations could be defined if you start counting one group of people relating to another group of people. These relations are typically termed cultural, religious or political and are generally outside the subject area of Generic Human Studies.

The "personal" relations are the ones you are in personally and involve only one other person. They are the Family, Social, and Work relations with a potential fourth category of Professional relations.

Each generic relation has a model or template of how each specific relation ideally operates.

The generic model of the ideal Parent/Child relation may not be the same as the personal Parent/Child relation you personally experienced.

Comparing the generic model of a specific Family, Social, or Work Relation helps you determine how successful you are/were in a personal experience of the generic relation.

Knowing to which type your relation exists is the first step when evaluating and analyzing your personal relations.

113. WHAT ARE THE GENERIC FAMILY RELATIONS?

The Family Relations contain the classic categories within a family as determined by genealogy, blood, and direct links through DNA.

The generic Family Relations are:

- Parent/Child Relation
- Sibling/Sibling Relation
- Grandparent/Grandchild Relation
- Kin/Kin Relation
- Adult Child/Aging Parent Relation

Family relations are not chosen. Your parents and their families represent a bigger system of which you're only a single part.

You may choose not to associate with your family members, but they are still your family.

114. What are the Generic Social Relations?

The Social Relations are non-blood, non-work associations created either by choice, marriage, or the environment.

The generic Social Relations are:

- Friend/Friend Relation
- Boyfriend/Girlfriend Relation
- Spouse/Spouse Relation
- In-law/In-law Relation
- Neighbor/Neighbor Relation

In general, humans choose social relations although some elements are more "chosen" than others.

For example, you might not know your neighbors when you move into a new area. But you did choose to move into that area. You may not have specifically chosen your "in-laws" but you certainly chose your spouse.

The social relations are also the source that creates new family relations, as in the Boyfriend/Girlfriend relations that evolve to become future Spouse/Spouse relations.

115. WHAT ARE THE GENERIC WORK RELATIONS?

Work Relations involve the people you work *with* not the people, such as customers or clients, you may interact with during your normal working hours.

The generic Work Relations are:

- Boss/Employee Relation
- Coworker/Coworker Relation

Work Relations involve the people with whom you work which are typically a Boss and/or your Employees if you are the Boss, and Coworkers.

You may have customers, or clients, or service people you deal with during the day. If so, these are not included in your personal Work Relations; these are best described as Professional Relations.

Work Relations are becoming an ever more important part of peoples' life, as more and more hours are dedicated to earning money. Many sacrifices are made from the Family and Social relations to feed the beast of Work relations.

116. What are the Generic "Professional" Relations?

A fourth type of relation exists for the roles that take place outside the "personal" category of relations.

Some generic Professional Relations are:

- Teacher/Student
- Doctor/Patient
- Repairman/Homeowner
- Accountant/Client
- Clerk/Customer
- Minister/Parishioner
- Lawyer/Client
- Politician/Constituent
- Police/Citizen

These relations typically involve the exchange of money outside of work. They make up the larger circle of human interactions typically affecting more than two people in some way usually with social, religious or political (governmental) oversight.

117. Why are "Professional" Relations Necessary?

Human society has evolved immensely from its more primitive days. In early human societies the tribe took care of everything. But as civilization has urbanized throughout the world there are too many tasks for everyone to learn for themselves so specialization has become necessary.

Professional relations are now a dominant aspect of the social structure of modern human society. They involve your needs outside the "personal" level of living. Depending upon how strong your society affects you, they can dictate much of your personal activities as a member of society.

118. How are "Professional" Relations Expanding?

"Professionals" often provide activities once considered social or leisure, such as daily shopping or dog walking. Why?

Typically you are a person with a "personal" need. If you are unable to meet your need in the "normal" way, such as walking your own dog, there is often a person who will specialize in meeting that need in exchange for money.

You have a dog but you never have time to take it for a walk. So you pay someone to do it. You have a lot of plants, but you don't have a green thumb or the time so you hire a service to come in once a week.

These relations often involve a specific service such as fixing things that go wrong with your body, home, work, or things you own and/or you just don't have the time and/or you make so much money it's worth it to you to pay someone to do these chores.

Chapter Ten:

How Do You Evaluate A Human Relation?

119. How Do You Evaluate a Specific Personal Relation?

The easiest way to evaluate a personal relation (one you are involved in) is to study the GHR Model for that relation. This would be the core structure of the generic relation with all its parts filled in with the proper detail.

Depending on which category of relation you want to study, its essential core will be based on the GHR model. Then the appropriate relation is simply filled in with the details specific to your situation.

As you study and work with the GHR relational model, you will eventually see a pattern in relations you never knew existed.

120. What Do You Mean By the "Generic Model" of a Relation?

The Generic Model of a relation is similar to the skeleton in the human body. It represents the structure upon which all relations are based. It serves as the skeleton of any relation without the flesh filled in.

Just like there are generic elements of a car, we have determined the generic elements of a relation. Once these parts are identified, then you would have a "model" of a relation.

Take for example, the Parent/Child Relation. All human societies have this relation and it operates in the same generic way within all cultures, religions, and political systems.

If you take a blank Generic Model of a relation, and fill in the details for the Parent/Child relation, you will then have the generic structure of a Parent/Child relation.

You can do the same with the Friend/Friend details, the Boss/Employee details, or any of the 12 relations. Every human relation is built from the same "generic structure" which consists of three parts.

121. What are the Three Parts of the Generic Model of Relations?

Every generic relation has three generic parts. Each part is completely distinct, yet mutually interdependent. Although distinct, each part must be present for the existence of the relation. Being able to distinguish and recognize these three parts is the first step in understanding how relations work.

The three parts of the relational model are always going to be:

- The Environment
- A Seesaw Structure
- Two Copartners

A relation only exists when these three parts are present and act in combination. Once you know how to separate and define these parts, much of the information and knowledge you already know about relations will fit right into place.

Every relation must contain these three elements. Even though each instance of a relation is unique, it is only unique because the conditions contained in the three parts are different.

122. What's an Easy Way to Memorize the Three Parts of a Generic Human Relation?

The easiest way to remember how a relation consists of three parts is to ask yourself what might be the three elements that make up a Children's Playground.

As you think about it you might realize there would need to be a patch of grass, or cement area, or some piece of property that was designated for the playground. This is the Environment.

For a playground to be a playground there must be some physical structures for the children to enjoy. This could be a slide or slippery dip, a swing set, perhaps even a seesaw, climbing gym or merry-go-round.

The final ingredient you'd need would be some children. If you had just a beautiful area with lots of structures, but no children, you still wouldn't have a functioning playground.

123. How Do You Define The Environment of a Relation?

The Environment is the physical setting and circumstances surrounding a relation. The interaction of any relation must take place within a specific environment, typically the immediate surroundings of the Two Copartners.

Examples of the Environment might be a home, school, work, a movie theater, or restaurant.

The Environment may be an integral part of the relational dynamics or simply a backdrop for the relational interaction. But without an Environment, there is no area within which the interaction of the relation can take place.

Assessing the Environment to see what part it might play in the success or failure of a specific relation can be an important diagnostic tool, one that is missing in many relation evaluation systems.

124. How Does the Environment Impact a Relation?

In terms of its affect on a specific relation, the Environment can help, hurt, or simply be a neutral backdrop for a relation's interaction.

If the Environment is extremely positive, this is an advantage. On the other hand it sometimes means a positive Environment could prop up an otherwise weak relation. If the Environment is hostile, a relation could experience a correspondingly difficult time.

For example, if a teacher or student is teaching or studying in a classroom with comfortable chairs, proper textbooks, and good lighting, the environment will support their progress. If they are in a broken-down classroom with terrible lighting, dilapidated chairs, and books that are ripped and missing pages, the environment will prove to be a negative influence.

The impact of the environment could also be major or minor. A Boyfriend/Girlfriend relation could take place against the neutral backdrop of a big city, small town, or even a foreign country. In any of these settings the relation would reflect the environment.

However, what if a Boyfriend/Girlfriend relation took place inside a prison? In this case the environment would have a distinctive impact on the relation.

125. What Are Some Other Ways the Environment Can Impact a Relation?

When the Copartners are separated by great distance, the environment can negatively affect the relation. In this situation you could say there is too much Environment.

Consider a marriage where both Copartners live in New York but one spouse is required to spend two weeks of every month in California. Although the marriage itself could be positive, the relation will still suffer due to the stressful circumstances of being separated for two weeks out of every month.

Another example of the Environment's influence could be shown in the Boss/Employee Relation. If the Employee works in an office adjacent to that of his/her Boss, the effect might be stressful. If the two offices were on different floors, for example, the effect could be more positive.

The physical environment at work can influence a work relation negatively or positively. One way this might be negative if the boss were so close he or she might have more opportunities to judge the employee negatively.

Alternatively, proximity could be positive if the boss got to know the employee better and learned to rely on him or her in emergency situations, and thus the employee might be promoted sooner.

126. What is the Structure of a Relation?

Every relation must be based on a structure. It is created by combination of two of society's roles, along with a set of rules and customs.

This structure creates the specific category of relation, as well as the basic premise and/or purpose the specific relation is meant to accomplish.

Think of this structure as similar to a seesaw, one plank but with two halves; one on either side of the fulcrum in the middle.

On a relational seesaw, you have one structure but two participants, one for each side of the seesaw. Each relational structure is named by combining the two roles that work together.

Some classic relational structures are named the Boss/Employee Structure, the Boyfriend/Girlfriend Structure, and the Parent/Child Structure.

127. WHAT ARE THE ROLES IN A RELATIONAL STRUCTURE?

A role specifies the instructions or guiding principles to be followed (by each human) playing that role in a relational category.

The name of the role summarizes, in an abbreviated form, the behaviors and instructions to be performed by each role. Generically speaking, the roles in relations are well defined. For example:

- The role of a Parent is to love, support, and nurture the Child
- The role of a Friend is to be supportive, spend time, and do things together
- The role of a Doctor is to diagnose the Patient's problem and to help him or her get well

Some relational structures have the same role on both sides of the seesaw, such as Friend/Friend Relation and Coworker/Coworker Relation.

The others have different roles, such as the Parent/Child Relation, Boyfriend/Girlfriend Relation, or Boss/Employee Relation.

128. How Do You Name a Relation?

A relation typically gets its name from the combination of the names of the two roles, such as the Parent/Child Relation, the Friend/Friend Relation, or the Boss/Employee Relation.

If the roles don't fit, then the relational structure isn't legitimate. For example, you couldn't have a Parent/Friend relation or a Boss/Neighbor relation.

129. How is a Role in a Relational Structure Different From the Human Copartner?

A role is a part to play, with defined expectations based on assuming that role. It is a completely separate and different entity from the person playing that role.

To help you understand this distinction, consider this example. The role of "Hamlet" is a famous acting role that everyone knows.

Many different actors (humans) have played this role. If someone playing Hamlet does a bad job, the critics don't blame the role of Hamlet; they blame the actor playing the role.

In the same way, if someone playing the Boss role or Parent role doesn't do a good job, you don't blame the Boss or Parent role itself; you blame the *person* playing that role.

The most important thing to remember about a role is that it is a separate, objective set of standards, all by itself. It exists as a concept in the outside world. It is not the human playing the part. All roles are positive and equal as balancing their respective structures. One role isn't "better" than the other.

The functionality of the role is always the same; however, different people will interpret a role differently, according to their own personality, skills, and abilities. Any role could have a positive or a negative expression of its dynamic by its Copartner.

130. What is the "Seesaw Analogy" of GHS?

As we've learned, a relational structure provides an objective standard or set of ideals for a purpose or goal. Although the structure of a relation is not an actual physical structure (like a seesaw), it is helpful if you begin thinking "as if" it were.

In GHS we use the shorthand of calling specific relations by their "seesaw" designation. Think of each combination of roles created by the relation as an objective plank for the two humans playing society's roles, just like a seesaw.

The Parent/Child Seesaw is one type of relation based on a specific purpose. The Boyfriend/Girlfriend Seesaw and Boss/Employee Seesaw are a second and third example.

131. How Does a Relation Function Like a "Seesaw?"

Suppose you are out walking by yourself and you come upon a children's play area where you recognize a seesaw, so you decide to sit down on one end.

After a while you realize nothing is happening so you decide if you go to the high end of the seesaw, it will be more exciting.

As you can imagine, the high part you are now on falls quickly to the ground, and the other end is now the high side.

It won't take long before you realize this seesaw structure is never going to work properly unless there is someone else sitting on the other side.

132. What Are Some More Ways a Relation Functions Like a "Seesaw?"

Suppose there was another person on the seesaw, but they weren't helping. They were just sitting there waiting for you to give them a ride. If you do all the pumping, this person will be happy, but he or she is not going to add one ounce of energy to help out.

You would soon find out that you'd have to do about twice as much work to keep this seesaw moving. To a casual observer it may appear to be a normal seesaw interaction. But the way that you feel working twice as hard to keep the seesaw moving doesn't feel exactly right.

What would happen if the two of you were actively making a seesaw work perfectly, and suddenly the other person decides to jump off without warning?

How would this seesaw function if your Copartner decided you weren't doing your job properly, so he/she came over to your side to show you how it's done? Or, he/she switched to a similar seesaw structure just like yours, but with another person?

As you can see, the "Seesaw Analogy" of GHS demonstrates the practical function of relations in many insightful ways.

Two people need to be on the right seesaw, on the same seesaw, for the same purpose, each on their own end.

If you perform your role on one side of a seesaw and the other person does not perform his or hers, then like a seesaw, the relation has no proper chance. One person can absolutely screw up a relationship built for two.

133. Who are the Two Copartners in a Relation?

The Two Copartners in GHR are the two humans playing specified roles on a relational Structure in a defined Environment.

They are the human flesh and blood, each with their three-part mind, playing the Parent role, Friend role, or Employee role, or whichever side of the identifiable relational structure they are on.

It always takes Two-Copartners to create a relation. Only one person on a relational seesaw means that it will not function correctly and indeed, it is not even considered a relation.

For the purpose of clarity we use the word "Two Copartners" together, to bring in the idea that it takes always and only two people, the Two Copartners, to make one personal relation function.

134. How Does Working With GHR Solve a Problem Relation?

If you are having a problem relation, the first practical step is to compare your personal relation to its generic standard. Once you can identify and evaluate how the function of your problem relation differs from its generic standard, you will know which areas to concentrate on to fix it.

Part of what the GHS smart-system does is to give you easier access to the true and useful information you already know about relations.

As you learn to focus your concentration on the three elements that matter most in a problem relation, you will often intuitively understand the source of the problem and how to resolve it.

When students of GHR diagnose what is truly wrong with a relation, they already know what steps to take to correct it. The reason the problem persisted was they were looking in the wrong area to solve the problem.

GHR can provide generic suggestions to improve your problem relations. Additionally, it can eliminate the false and non-useful information you may be acting on, which has kept you from seeing what is really going on with your personal relations.

It may also be the cause of your problem lies strictly with the other Copartner. If this is so, you will need the cooperation of your Copartner to repair the relation, or else it is doomed.

135. What Do We Know About Relations So Far?

What we now know in the simplest terms is that every relation takes place:

- IN an Environment
- ON a Seesaw Structure
- BETWEEN 2 Copartners

136. How Can a Relation Be Evaluated With Such a Simple Explanation of How Relations Work?

We know about the three main elements that create a relation, but wouldn't there have to be more to the GHR system than this? The answer is yes.

One problem at this point is we don't yet have enough details pertaining to each part of the generic relational model to evaluate a specific relation.

Each main element of a relation is composed of three smaller sub-parts. Once you decide which element of the relation you want to evaluate, you then go to its three subparts to get more specific details.

Now that you know the basic model of GHR, we can take a deeper look at each of the sub-parts for the Environment, Structure, and Two Copartners.

Chapter Eleven:

What Is a Deeper Level of the Environment?

137. What is a Deeper Level of Understanding the Environment?

Each environment is composed of three subparts, which facilitate a deeper evaluation of the environmental element. These three subparts combine to create the total picture of the environment:

- Location (where the relation takes place)
- Duration (how long the Copartners have been on the specific relation structure)
- Timing (the time of day the Copartners interact, including how much time they spend together at a time, and how many times they interact during a set period of time.)

Let's explore each of these three aspects of the Environment in greater detail.

138. What is a Specific Understanding of the Location?

Location refers to the physical boundaries of the relation's activity. Where does the action of a relation take place? How far can the Copartners see around them?

Do four walls, wide-open spaces, or the inside of a car surround them? Is the action in a foxhole with hand grenades bursting around? Are the Two Copartners sipping drinks while dining in a fancy restaurant? Are the Two Copartners in a classroom, stuck in an elevator, or 240 miles above the earth?

The features of the Location play a crucial role in determining a relation's positive or negative qualities. Many people have been involved in a mutually nourishing relation, only to have some aspect of the Location change, making the relation impossible to continue.

One example might be two people who meet while vacationing in Hawaii. Perhaps they met on the plane and discover they live in the same city.

Now the romantic Hawaiian nights and the fact that neither is working allow time for a romantic relation to evolve and grow stronger.

They might thoroughly enjoy those 7 days in Hawaii. But when they return home they could discover the realities of their primary locations are not conducive to continuing the relation.

139. How Do You Determine the Location of a Relation?

To establish the Location of any relation, just describe the external surroundings where the Copartners interact.

Is it the beach, the library, Wisconsin, a laundromat, a playground, work cafeteria, or where?

Then, if there are any specific aspects of this location out of the ordinary, make a mental note of this as well.

For example, perhaps the relation takes place in a grocery store, but only during the hours it's closed because both Copartners are stock-replacement employees.

If some aspect of the location is different or unusual, it's advisable to ascertain if it impacts the precise relation in any major way.

140. What is a Specific Understanding of Duration?

Duration refers to the total length of time the Copartners have been involved. In other words, when did this relation start?

How long have both Copartners been together on this specific relational seesaw?

The Duration of some relations, such as the Clerk/Customer relation, may only last a few minutes; others, such as the Sibling/Sibling relation, can last for decades.

One factor to keep in mind is Duration is specific to a defined seesaw structure. An example might be two Coworkers who have been working together for two years. But then they start dating. So, the Duration for their Boyfriend/Girlfriend seesaw begins from the point they embarked on their first date.

141. What is a Specific Understanding of Timing in the Environment?

Timing refers primarily to the time of day the relation interaction takes place and how much time the Two Copartners spend together. It also includes how many times the Two Copartners interact within a specific time period.

Timing is often a critical factor in the experience of a relation. For example, the Timing for a female jogging alone in Central Park would have different implications at ten o'clock in the morning as opposed to ten o'clock at night.

Most work relations have Timing that takes place during the day. However, a significant number of work relations have Timing that occurs at night, which contributes environmental stress and strain to the job.

Timing also refers to the length of time the Copartners spend interacting with each other. Is it 5 minutes, 5 hours, 5 days, or 5 months?

Time also can be important based on how many times in a day/week/month the Two Copartners interact.

In the Parent/Child relation the environmental aspect of Timing would be extremely different for the Child who interacts with his/her Parent intermittently for twenty minutes to two hours each day as opposed to the child who's Timing is two weekends a month with the Parent.

The difference between the two Timings can tell you much about the different experience of the two Parent/Child relations.

142. What is an Interesting Example of the Environment's Impact on a relation?

The importance of the environment can be illustrated by sharing an example that came up during a seminar on Generic Human Studies.

One student stood up and said she was having a terrible time of it with her Boss/Employee relation and asked what she should do? She said that she didn't know why she was having the problem, but she was quitting her job on Monday because she just couldn't stand it anymore.

Thinking it was her boss, the seminar moderator asked her, "Why do you hate your Boss?" She replied, "I don't. I love my Boss, he's great."

Thinking it had to be the structure, and she just didn't like her job duties, the moderator said, "You must hate what you're doing." She replied, "Oh no, I love my job. It's fantastic. I just have to quit."

By this time, everyone in the room was confused! Why was this employee quitting her job on Monday when she loved her Boss so much as well the work she was doing?

143. How Can an Atypical Environment Affect a Copartner's Experience in a relation?

The answer, completely unbeknownst to the employee, turned out to be the Environment. She was in a proper Boss/Employee structure with a Copartner she really liked.

However, the Environment of her job was at her Boss's home, an atypical Environment for a generic work relation.

Because of the Location where she was doing normal work, (typing, answering the phone, etc), she found herself expected to do things like walk her Boss's dog, pick up dry cleaning, and take abusive messages from the ex-wife.

This mixing of her duties caused by the home Location of the business resulted in her resenting her work experience.

She realized she was unhappy; so, quite unconsciously her gut reaction was to quit without even knowing why.

She knew it wasn't her boss or the proper work itself. Because she didn't know the real reason why she was unhappy, and couldn't point to anything specific, her solution was to leave thinking it was "just her."

144. How Does Recognizing a Problem in the Environment Help a Copartner?

Once the unhappy employee understood what was happening, she decided to discuss the situation with her Boss to see what could be done.

As it turned out, he was very sympathetic and understood completely. She consequently had new enthusiasm and energy to continue working there, despite the difficulties presented by the location.

Once she was aware of the situation, she could keep an eye on her job duties to make sure they were work-related, not personal or home-related for her Boss. Even her Boss agreed she was not obligated or expected to perform household duties.

Becoming familiar with the generic Environments for each relational structure helps a Copartner recognize and evaluate potential problems possibly affecting him or her in an atypical or even typical situation.

145. What is the Key to the Environment's Impact on a relation?

The Environment can have a dramatic impact on any relation, or just be the incidental back-drop for the interaction. Although the Environment is usually the easiest to determine and assess, most people don't take the time or have the tools to evaluate it consciously. They just take it for granted.

Now you know how to evaluate the key components of any Environment. Once you've determined the Location, Duration, and Timing of a specific relation, along with any variations, it is easy to assess the positive or negative impact of the environment.

Positive relations typically take place in an Environment that is nurturing and supportive.

They take place in an accommodating location, over a duration necessary to support the needs and goals of the Two Copartners, and during the appropriate times of the day (or night).

If any factor in the Location, Duration, or Timing is negative, this creates a negative influence on the relational interaction.

Chapter Twelve:

What is A Deeper Level Of the Structure?

146. What are the Deeper Levels of a Structure?

The 12 generic relational "seesaws" are the structures we explore most closely in Generic Human Studies.

Although we know the 12 structures, we do need more detail to evaluate the specifics of each different structure. You will have this capability when you learn the subparts that make up a structure. They are:

- Roles
- Rules
- Customs

Every relational structure always contains two sets of Roles, two sets of Rules, and two sets of Customs, one for each side of the seesaw.

When the roles are the same, as in the Friend/Friend or Neighbor/Neighbor structures, there are two separate, identical and equal sets of Roles, Rules, and Customs.

If the relational seesaw structure has different roles, such as Boss/Employee or Husband/Wife, then the Roles, Rules, and Customs are also different.

147. How Do You Identify the Different Roles?

To keep track of the many varieties of roles, we can assign each into one of the three primary types:

- Family
- Social
- Work

Each type of relation has its own group of associated roles.

148. What are Some of the Different Family Roles?

Some examples of specific Family Roles are:

- Mother
- Father
- Daughter
- Son
- Sister
- Brother
- Grandparent
- Grandchild
- Aunt/Uncle
- Cousins
- Nephew/Niece
- Adult Child
- Aging Parent

149. What are Some of the Different Social Roles?

Some examples of specific Social Roles are:

- Best Friend
- Friend
- Acquaintance
- Girlfriend
- Boyfriend
- Husband
- Wife
- Mother-in-law
- Father-in-law
- Sibling-in-law
- Daughter-in-law
- Son-in-law
- Neighbor

150. What are Some of the Different Work Roles?

The Work Roles are:

- Boss
- Employee
- Coworker

151. What is a Summarized Understanding of Roles?

ROLES are the set of social expectations associated with each half of a relation.

Although there are many possible roles to play in the varieties of available relations, only certain roles can go together to create a proper seesaw structure.

Certain roles naturally go together, and these combinations create the 12 classic relational structures as outlined in Chapter Nine.

For example, there would not be a relation such as a Wife/Friend Structure. It's either the Husband/Wife Structure or the Friend/Friend Structure.

We've already discussed roles in detail forming the two sides of the seesaw. We also know they represent a one-word description summarizing the expected social behavior required for that relation.

When defining a role, we use a one-sentence description to encapsulate a specific set of social expectations associated with the role. The name for the list of social expectations defined by the Role turns out to be the next relational subpart.

152. WHAT IS A SPECIFIC UNDERSTANDING OF RULES?

Rules are the specific collection of detailed instructions that pertain to each relation's role. While a role is best described in one sentence, there can and will be many rules that apply to each different role.

Rules are the full list of appropriate and expected behaviors that exemplify each Role. Some Roles have a limited number of Rules, while the more important Roles have a long list of prescribed behaviors and duties.

Rules define the expected behavior for the person playing the role. Rules offer the quickest, easiest, and most effective way of performing the tasks associated with a role.

In fact, you can say that if you are following the Rules for a role, you are performing the role properly. Knowing and following the Rules of each relational Role is a specific key to more effective relational skills.

Following the Rules builds the strength of a relation. Breaking the Rules weakens and eventually destroys the relation.

153. What are Some Specific Examples of Rules?

Some examples of Rules for the Parent Role might be:

- Feed the child
- Make sure the child wears clean clothes to school
- Help the child with his/her homework

Some examples of Rules for the Neighbor Role might be:

- Don't play loud music after 11 o'clock at night
- Don't leave the garbage bin out all week
- Mow your lawn regularly

Rules for the Friend Roles might be:

- Don't repeat stories told in confidence
- Share expenses equally when going out
- Return phone calls when your friend calls you

154. Are Rules Positive or Negative in a Relation?

Technically speaking, Rules are instructions and in this sense they are neutral.

Rules can be written with a positive slant, such as "Always tell the truth." or in the negative such as, "Never lie."

It also could be that a person playing a Role doesn't want to follow the Rules, so he or she could infer Rules as being negative.

However, Rules are actually the tests that reveal if you, or a person you are on a relational seesaw with, are being positive in a relation. In this sense, they are the scorecard used to identify and define each relation's Role.

Because there could be so many rules associated with a structure, it's best to list them according to the specific relation. GHS maintains a full list of the generic rules for each relational structure.

155. HOW CAN YOU DEFINE A MORE SPECIFIC CLASSIFICATION OF RULES?

Some relational roles can have 40 Rules or more. This creates a very long list of Rules without some way of categorizing the choices.

In Generic Human Studies we use a simple way to identify a rule category. This makes it very helpful for easy referral when searching for the exact rule in a role.

Once you have defined a role, its Rules are put into one of the following four (PEMS) categories:

- Physical Rules
- Emotional Rules
- Mental Rules
- Social Rules

156. WHAT ARE PHYSICAL RULES?

Physical Rules involve basic nuts-and-bolts practical things. Some typical Physical Rules for a Parent Role are:

- Feed the baby
- Change wet diapers
- Keep an eye on the baby while it plays

Physical rules for the Employee Role are:

- Start work on time
- Answer the phone on the second ring
- Don't steal money

Physical Rules involve the physical environment and define specific physical instructions intended to fulfill the physical purpose or function of a role.

157. What are Emotional Rules?

Emotional Rules have more to do with the feeling/emotive aspects of a role.

A set of sibling rules might include:

- Maintain communication through telephone or email
- Show emotional support
- Acknowledge birthdays

Some emotional rules for a Boss role might be:

- Have a helpful and supportive attitude
- Keep an Employee's confidences private
- Listen to an Employee's problems or complaints without reacting personally

Emotional rules govern the impact a Copartner can have on the emotional environment and well-being of the second Copartner performing the matching role. They involve each other's feelings and emotional comforts.

158. What are Mental Rules?

Mental rules are concerned with teaching, learning, and the mental/moral portion of performing a relational role.

Mental rules for a Friend structure might be:

- Ask for personal advice
- Teach and share information
- Do not withhold important information

Mental rules for a Coworker Role might be:

- Express and defend your ideas
- Do not discuss personal details of another Coworker's life
- Follow the work performance guidelines

Mental rules involve the logistics and thinking aspects related to the performance of a role in a relation. Logic, sequence & causality, and third-party verifiability are mental concepts.

159. What are Social Rules?

Social rules involve your behavior within a personal relation (Parent/Child, Friend/Friend, Boss/Employee, etc) as it relates to outside people or social situations you may encounter in concurrence with your personal relation.

For example, if you were the boyfriend, you would be expected to attend the wedding of your girlfriend's sister, especially if she were in the bridal party. This would be a social expectation held by others.

A social rule at work might be that you are expected to attend the company picnic and be part of the softball team playing against other divisions in the company.

Social Rules are designed to "play nice" with others in group situations and seek to reduce the social stress levels for others in society.

160. What is a Summarized Understanding of Rules?

Because there can be a variety of relational Rules, it's helpful to use the four descriptors of Physical, Emotional, Mental, and Social Rules to help identify and categorize all the various rules.

Using PEMS is a specific tool of the GHS Smart-System, as it helps the USER to "drill down" to a core area of concern for evaluation.

161. WHAT IS A SPECIFIC UNDERSTANDING OF CUSTOMS?

Customs, the third subpart of a relation structure, are the specific cultural, and/or religious, and/or political mores associated with a role relative to the specific country, religion, or political system under which you grew up or live within currently.

One of the reasons people think relations are so hard to evaluate is because there are so many different customs associated with any one type of relation. Even the study of sociology has various methods to study, categorize, and catalog the variations of human customs.

The fact different human societies have so many variable customs associated with a specific relation does not change the core Roles and Rules of the relation's structure.

162. How Can You Keep Track of All the Customs in Human Society?

The short answer is "we don't even try."

Each society has a multitude of specific customs to accompany it's version of the 12 standard Structures.

The Customs section of a relation role could never be generic, since so many differences in customs exist within the different human societies.

The component of Customs is the part of the Structure that accommodates all the social, religious, and political differences in the generic relational roles. Here is the specific place to identify and put any specific customs that might be affecting a personal relation you wish to evaluate.

163. How are Customs Used in Evaluating Personal relations?

We need to know where to place the potentially dramatic differences that can occur when a cross-cultural relation is being evaluated.

Customs can easily be the trouble spot when two people of differing nationalities or religions engage in an important relation, since each person will have culture-based expectations of the other's roles and rules.

Typically these are unconscious expectations that "are obvious" but ONLY if you are part of that cultural expectation.

Each Copartner may be doing what is right for his or her Role according to his/her culture, but their actions could easily confuse, hurt, or even insult the other person because of cultural or religious expectations from the other person's world.

For example, all cultures recognize the Husband/Wife structure as a key social relation. The fact that members of one culture jump over a broom to proclaim their marriage while others walk under an arch reflects a Custom.

If you find yourself arguing with your future spouse over some specific Customs in your wedding plans, then it's good to know where this fits and what kinds of problems for which to watch.

164. What is So Important About Customs if They are Not Generic?

Customs are often the first undeniable clue that there may be potential problems for a long-term intimate relation.

Customs are extremely important to the members of a society or group. They serve to code and communicate various ideals and meanings shared with other members. In fact, customs are a way of differentiating one's culture from other societies, and thus form a basis for claiming identity or uniqueness.

They are also part of a very personal fabric disclosing how that culture or society evolved from its past ancestors. By maintaining their customs, a group of people can establish their identity as a society unique and apart from any other.

In Generic Human Studies analysis, the specific customs of your relation are the least important factor as far as comparing your personal relation to its generic counterpart.

However, Customs may be specifically where a conflict between Two Copartners resides. If so, this is where you have to look to determine why and how much these Customs are affecting your relation. It is very difficult to maintain a intimate relation with strong cultural, religious, or political differences

165. How Can You Keep Track of So Many Customs?

There are many, many human Customs that are specific to generic relations. You would have great difficulty attempting to catalog all the relation Customs for the many different groups of human society that have ever existed.

Luckily, in GHS you don't have to do that. What you do have to remember is to evaluate the Customs relevant to you and your Copartner for the seesaw structure you are on.

This section of Customs is where you put the cultural, religious, or political practices important enough to affect the roles of a personal relation.

For example, let's say a Jewish person marries an Islamic person. The generic relational structure would be the Husband/Wife seesaw. But the differing cultural and religious Customs accorded to their Husband/Wife roles will have plenty of potential for conflict.

In this situation, Customs are predicted to be the most active area of friction between the couple.

And even if the couple were comfortable with their differences (as romantic couples often are in the beginning), their respective family and relatives would undoubtedly have problems condoning their marriage, which would inevitably place additional pressure on the relation.

166. What are Cultural Customs?

Your culture typically implies your race, gender, age, religion, and country of origin, all things that existed before you were born. By the virtue of your birth you became a member automatically and irrevocably of this culture and no other.

Let's assume you were born into the above culture and lived in it for 10-20 years. This experience would now be part of your mental conditioning. Even if you moved away you would carry the expectations of your culture.

Thornleigh, Australia, in 1998, for the Lebanese children who had grown up there after their parents emigrated, was experientially the same as if it were Lebanon in 1958. Why?

Because when their parents immigrated to Australia, they continued to follow and maintain the same customs from their small village in Lebanon as if it was still 1958. Many of these westernized Lebanese Australians were going back to Lebanon to marry someone from their same village.

When they went back to actual Lebanon, they found their similar aged counterparts, to be living in a more relaxed and modern social culture than their lives in Australia.

167. How Does the Influence of Culture Help the Two Copartners?

Customs are influenced by the culture in which you live or were raised, the religious customs associated with your beliefs, and the political system where you live.

When Two Copartners in a relation follow the same cultural, religious, and political customs, they simply go along with the prescribed customs of their dominant relational structure as if it was the most normal thing in the world.

It's also understood in Generic Human Studies that whatever culture you grew up in will be your first choice for best culture.

168. What are Some Specific Examples of Differing Customs?

If you live in the United States, but were born into a large Turkish family, it is likely your immediate local Turkish community would have the dominant influence on the way you live your life, even if you live in the U.S.

Perhaps from this same family you grew up in the U.S., but then you move back to Turkey. In this situation you will have yet another set of social expectations governing your behavior in regards to the 12 generic relational structures.

Age can also be a factor in customs. Teens often create mini-societies, where their music and entertainment customs establish who they are and what they stand for. An example of this might be the "Surfers" versus the "Goths" versus the "Jocks" who exclude each other in high school society (as codified in Hollywood movies).

If a specific custom important to you is a result of your up-bringing, social ties, or the country you grew up in, then it goes under the category of customs, which by definition is not generic.

169. Where Do Cultural Customs Come From?

Societies evolve their customs from the land surrounding their country as well as language, religion, and political sensitivities. Sometimes these customs have remained relevant for centuries.

Societies and cultures in this modern age of global communications have a way of changing more quickly. Economic realities are also part of this equation.

What if you grew up during the Great Depression of the 30s? This will have a strong bearing on the way you consume resources and how you choose to spend your money.

You will certainly have a vastly different set of social expectations for your spending habits than a person growing up in the USA during the 1980s, when conspicuous consumption was the goal.

If you grew up in a rural area, your customs could be completely different to a similar person growing up in your same country's largest city.

Customs can vary in many ways. They are important as they influence the decisions you make in the various relations you choose.

170. What relations Need to Worry Most About Cultural Customs?

The relations most likely to bring problems involving Customs are the Social type. Families typically share customs, and earning money at work is a separate distinction. Mixing with "strangers" is where worlds can collide.

Customs are most likely to affect the intimate social relations between Two Copartners of different race, religion, or even political parties.

Since this is relatively rare compared to the cultural average, it doesn't come up as often. However, as more and more citizens of different cultures are being exposed to each other in various ways, these problems will increase.

When customs contain the prediction of conflict, as in the Husband/Wife or In-law/In-law examples mentioned earlier, conflict and tension from family members on both sides is assured.

So it's not only important, it's mandatory to have a Customs section when evaluating your personal human relations, especially if they are cross-cultural.

171. What are Religious Customs?

Possibly the strongest and most deeply held customs are religious, especially when they are reinforced and held in place by cultural and political customs.

You may have grown up in a country where everyone is a member of the same religion and all the political policies are derived from this religion.

You could also have grown up without a strong religion, in a country where few cultural or political customs were inspired by religious beliefs.

So depending upon your specific circumstances, religious customs may or may not be a factor for you. However, they could be very important for the person with whom you are in a relation. If you discover there are religious customs which create a conflict within a personal relation, list them in this section.

What would be the pertinent religious customs if a Jewish man married a Muslim woman? What might be the important religious customs if a Muslim male married a Jewish woman? Would they differ? Which century might we be discussing during this dialogue? How might the dynamics of this relation change for the couple based on living in Israel as opposed to living in one of the various Muslim countries?

172. What are Political Customs?

Political Customs are more in the territory of state-mandated policies or specific governmental solutions for dealing with and managing members of society. Another example might be that fireworks are a custom of the July 4 celebrations of the US Independence Day.

You could have Democratic customs vs. Republican customs. You could have American customs vs. Chinese customs, or French, or Sudanese.

These often reflect an opinion about how society should work and be governed, and who should pay for what and why.

A strong example of political customs overriding the generic normal is China's one-child policy. Most cultures would let its members have as many children as they like. But in China, the political state has mandated this change.

Suppose you analyzed a Boyfriend/Girlfriend relation between a Uruguayan female and an American male living in Australia. There could be numerous ways the various customs from any of the three countries could impact the generic Boyfriend/Girlfriend structure.

If you agree with or follow a custom because of the country, laws, or the political system under which you were raised, it is called a political custom.

173. WHY IS IT IMPORTANT TO DEFINE THE STRUCTURE OF A RELATION BETWEEN TWO COPARTNERS?

A confusing situation can exist when Two Copartners happen to be on more than one relational seesaw. A classic example of this is when a son works for his father. Most people approach this situation as only one relation.

However, the Two Copartners are actually on two separate Structures, the Parent/Child seesaw and the Boss/Employee seesaw. If you ask either of the Copartners if there is something wrong, they may say yes, the relation is having problems, but which relation? Copartners often entangle the assigned rules associated with their two different roles.

If the Son was only on a Boss/Employee structure, then things might proceed smoothly. He would act as an Employee and follow the rules that represent how an Employee would act.

However, if the Father has a son as an Employee, he might have trouble keeping the two relational seesaws separate. He might expect his son to work in a different manner or with a different attitude than the typical employee. Or he may discuss a personal family issue during the workday.

It's very easy for the same Two Copartners on double seesaws to confuse their two separate roles. This often causes problems that hurt both relations.

174. WHAT EXAMPLE SHOWS A TRULY COMPLEX ENMESHMENT OF STRUCTURES BETWEEN COPARTNERS IN "ONE" RELATION?

One excellent example of structural enmeshment comes from a married couple who attended one of the GHR seminars. They originally attended the class because they thought they were having problems with "their marriage" (as well as their mutual boss), and wanted to "work it out."

During the seminar they discovered they were actually on each of the following relational seesaws:

- Husband/Wife (This they knew.)
- Parent/Child (They had a one-year-old child, which adds two more structures, Mother/Son and Father/Son.)
- Boss/Employee (For certain duties, the wife was the husband's boss.)
- Coworker/Coworker (A percentage of the time they were Coworkers working together under their boss.)
- Boss/Employee (two more Boss/Employee structures with both as employees of their boss.)
- Landlord/Tenants (It turns out their mutual boss was also their landlord.)
- Landlord/Manager (The husband also managed the apartment complex for their boss in partial exchange for rent. These last two are professional relations.)

Add all this to the environmental oddity that all these relations took place at the same location. This couple lived upstairs above their job location, were working in a non-typical work environment (an apartment running a book publishing business), and were sharing nine different relational structures all within the same environment. Can you see how this couple might have thought they were having "trouble with their marriage?"

Once this couple understood their total relational experiences actually included all these various seesaw structures, they learned how to step back and determine which structure they were on at any given time.

They were then able to start resolving conflicts by behaving appropriately for the specific structure they were on at the time.

For example, when they knew they were on the Coworker/Coworker structure they behaved differently than when they were on the Husband/Wife structure.

Both Copartners intuitively "knew" which behavior was appropriate for which role; they had just never realized how many different Structures they were actually on.

After applying GHR to their situation, this couple was easily able to appreciate and manage these distinctions in the "real world" in exactly the same environment with exactly the same Co-partners.

175. How Does Knowing About A Relation's Structure Help in Evaluating a relation?

Understanding the three parts of the Structure (roles/rules/customs) helps when evaluating the deeper levels of a problem relation.

For example, you might have to decide if a person is violating the Role of a relational Structure, or just breaking one of its Rules. Or you might anticipate that Two Copartners from contrasting cultures would experience conflict with each other's Customs when involved in a social or business relation.

When you want to evaluate how a relation is working, you must classify the specific type of relational structure you are evaluating. The three subparts exist to help you establish the differences between each relation.

The three subparts of Roles, Rules, and Customs, are always going to be part of the objective structure, but each subpart will be filled with different information according to the type of relation.

There is a big difference between a Boyfriend/Girlfriend Structure and a Husband/Wife Structure. There is a big difference between a Parent/Child Structure and a Boss/Employee Structure.

In fact, each of the 12 classic relational Structures is completely different. It is the seesaw element of the relational model that defines these distinctions.

Chapter Thirteen:

What is A Deeper Level of The Two-Copartners?

176. WHAT IS A DEEPER LEVEL OF UNDERSTANDING THE TWO COPARTNERS?

Next, we are going to take a deeper look at the third element needed to establish a relation as well as its most complex, the Two Copartners.

More specifically, the two humans we call the Two Copartners. These are the people playing the two roles of the seesaw structure; otherwise known as "sitting on the seesaw."

It's been fairly simple to outline the Environment, and just a bit more complicated to outline the Structure of the Generic Relational Model.

The question now is how do we judge a person's behavior while on the seesaw, considering all the possible variables?

The key is to look at each person, not strictly as an individual, but as to how well they perform their role (follow the rules) on their side of the seesaw.

One person might have a great personality, above average intelligence, and even display a sense of humor, but be a lousy Copartner in a specific relation.

Perhaps the majority of people would evaluate a specific person negatively, but in one particular relation he or she might do all the right things. So in this relation he or she will be an excellent Copartner.

177. What Three Subparts Help Define the Two Copartners' Element of a relation?

Copartners also have three subparts to enable a deeper evaluation of their participation in a relation. Each Copartner playing the role in a relation can be evaluated based on his or her:

- Traits
- Needs
- Tactics

A Copartner's particular combination of Traits, Needs, and Tactics represents an excellent predictor of his/her ability to play a specific relation's Role.

It's as simple as this. The more a person has positive Traits, Needs, and Tactics, the better he or she will play the Role.

The more a person has negative Traits, Needs, and Tactics, the worse he or she will play the Role.

Because there are two roles for each structure, there are two Copartners needed to play each role. So each Copartner is assessed based on their unique combination of Traits, Needs, and Tactics.

178. What are a Copartner's Traits?

Traits are specific aspects or elements of a person's personality. Any one person could have hundreds of traits in a completely different combination from the next person.

Individual traits can be positive, such as having humor, being good-looking, or smart. Or they could be negative, such as being arrogant, lazy, or dishonest. Traits could even be neutral, such as hair color or height.

A person's traits are deep elements of his/her personality, which consequently can be difficult to change.

Using the GHS system we evaluate the traits that specifically outline how each person participates in a relation.

It's a simple system. If a Copartner has positive traits, that's good. If he or she has negative traits, that's bad.

179. What Traits are the Most Important When "Relating" in a relation?

Although every person has a wide variety of personality traits, seven main traits are used to evaluate specifically how a person acts (and reacts) on a relational seesaw. These are:

- Being Attracted
- Being Committed
- Being Genuine
- Being Trustworthy
- Being Emotionally Mature
- Having Communication Skills
- Having Problem-Solving Skills

These seven traits predict how a person will perform any role on his or her side of the seesaw.

If a Copartner is positive in all seven Traits, he or she will perform well in their role; conversely, if these seven Traits of a person are negative, this Copartner will sabotage any relation.

Another aspect of traits is that they are relation-specific. In other words, a Copartner's Traits are expressed within the context of a specific relational structure. A good example of this is the first trait we will examine.

180. Why is "Being Attracted" the First Trait to Evaluate on a relational Seesaw?

"Being Attracted" is the trait of having a strong feeling or sense of connection toward the other Copartner.

Without this attraction, a Copartner won't be able to sustain the relation because he or she will not "stay on the seesaw."

Ideally, this sense of connection is felt by both Copartners.

If one (or especially both) of the Copartners on the relational seesaw lacks the trait of Being Attracted, the bond of the relation will be too one-sided to succeed without severe problems.

181. What are Some Aspects of "Being Attracted?"

The trait of Being Attracted has different characteristics for particular relational structures.

For example, in most romantic relations, the trait of Being Attracted typically starts with the sexual chemistry of how great-looking you think the other person is. As the relation progresses, deeper elements of Being Attracted to the person come into play.

In a work relation, such as Boss/Employee, Being Attracted has an entirely different focus.

Here as the Employee, you might be attracted to your boss based on his or her expertise or experience in a particular area. Working with that person might be the best possible way to learn and progress in your career. You are happy and excited to be on the Boss/Employee seesaw with this person.

As a Boss, you might be attracted to an Employee who is anxious to learn, and motivated to succeed. This way, you can mentor him or her, passing on your knowledge and experience.

On the other hand, as an Employee, your urgent need for money right now might make you attracted to any Boss who will give you a job.

If you are a Boss and your secretary quit yesterday, you might consider "Being Attracted" to anyone who can type over 50 words a minute and use a spell checker.

Another example might be that you have three or four potential neighbor relations, but you find yourself "attracted to" only one particular neighbor for some reason.

Maybe they have a similar education as you, your children are the same age, or they play the same sports as you. Thus, you are potentially more motivated to establish a relation with them.

This trait of Being Attracted is a bit tricky to grasp in the beginning. However, the bottom line is two individual humans must be attracted enough to each other to be willing to sit on the same seesaw structure long enough to see if a relation is even possible.

If neither person is "Being Attracted" to the other, within the context of the seesaw structure, there is no "glue" binding them together on the seesaw.

182. What are Some Aspects of "Being Committed?"

The trait of "Being Committed" is the second measure of how much time and energy a person is willing to invest on a seesaw structure.

It is also the guarantee each Copartner gives the other insuring he/she will remain in the relation.

Being committed means giving time and energy to the relation, and in life each Copartner only has so much time and energy to go around. Therefore, a Copartner's trait of Being Committed is a crucial characteristic of his/her intentions.

Another aspect of Being Committed is how motivated each Copartner is to meet the other's needs. If only one Copartner acts to meet the needs of the other, the long-term value of the relation will suffer.

Ideally, each Copartner contributes a balanced amount of time and energy (Commitment) to their relation, even if this energy assumes different forms. For example, in a Work relation one Copartner might put in 90% of the time and the other 90% of the money, but the contribution of energy could be considered equal by both sides.

If one Copartner puts in a disproportionate amount of time or energy, the relation will be unbalanced, and this portends potential problems. What happens if only one person on a seesaw attempts to do the work for both sides?

That person becomes very tired, and the relation will not be successful.

183. What are Some Aspects of "Being Genuine?"

The trait of "Being Genuine" is the willingness and honesty each person has to communicate his/her true thoughts, feelings, and needs. Being Genuine in relations is appreciated by other Copartners more than any other quality.

Copartners must be willing to be honest with one another. If a Copartner expresses false opinions or values, the relation is based on pretense only.

If one Copartner tries to camouflage his/her true thoughts, feelings, or needs, the relation can only suffer. If both Copartners conceal their thoughts, feelings, or needs from each other, the relation will be superficial at best.

Genuine Copartners will not hide their thoughts, feelings, or needs, nor will they waste energy creating facades. They will not be evasive in conversation, nor would they distort the facts about their job, accomplishments, income, age, marital status, or other aspects of their life.

184. What are Some Aspects of "Being Trustworthy?"

The trait of "Being Trustworthy" is the potential that each Copartner has to depend upon each other. This trait provides the basis for building trust, which is an essential aspect of exchanging needs.

If Copartners can't trust each other riding on the relational seesaw, how relaxed and comfortable will they feel? The betrayal of trust is the ruin of any relation.

Trustworthy Copartners will not reveal information given in confidence nor later use this information against the other. Nor do they criticize each other in public.

Once trust has been established, trustworthy Copartners will be open and honest about any condition or fact in their lives.

The Roles of every relational structure come alive when they are played by Two Copartners who are trustworthy.

185. What are Some Aspects of "Being Emotionally Mature?"

The trait of "Being Emotionally Mature" is the ability of a Copartner to balance his/her personal needs against the relational needs of the other person. If either person is immature, their overriding concern for meeting their own needs will hurt the relation over the long term.

Emotionally Mature Copartners maintain a balanced perspective of needs within a relation. They understand their own needs and motives and are aware of and sensitive to the needs and motives of the other Copartner.

They recognize the importance of a relation's structure and concentrate on nurturing and protecting it. They also reject the formation of relations with Copartners having negative traits.

Emotionally Mature Copartners have a positive sense of self-esteem, which includes self-caring and self-sufficiency. Since they recognize and understand their priorities, they use their energy and skills in a positive and fulfilling manner.

Emotionally Mature Copartners are interested in enjoying and improving their relation. Thus, they will expend energy to achieve that purpose. Reading this book is a good example.

186. What are Some Aspects of "Having Communication Skills?"

The trait of "Having Communication Skills" is the ability of a Copartner to share and express his/her personal thoughts, feelings, and needs.

People think, feel, and have needs, but this does not necessarily mean they can communicate them to others.

If one Copartner can accurately communicate what he/she is thinking, feeling, and needing to the other person, then the communication has a chance to be received the way it was intended. It's also important that the other Copartner have the communication skills to be able to listen and correctly interpret the communication from the other Copartner.

The condition of the Two Copartners both Having Communication Skills helps to prevent problems and keep the relation free of stress.

One of the best ways to insure a relation's success is for the Copartners to be continually communicating and working to improve their communication skills. In this way, problem areas for one or both Copartners won't become stuck, thus becoming a permanent part of the relational dynamics.

187. What are Some Aspects of "Having Problem-Solving Skills?"

The trait of "Having Problem-Solving Skills" is the ability and willingness to resolve problems within a relation. Relations are a union, and unresolved conflict will cause the union to weaken and eventually crumble.

Since no relation can be without conflict, Problem-Solving skills are essential to facilitate a relation running smoothly. The style of Problem-Solving used by a Copartner will have a strong impact on the functioning of the relation.

Copartners with positive Traits realize most problems in a relation are created by unmet needs.

They understand the way to avoid problems is to communicate their needs honestly and openly with their Copartner on a regular basis.

However, if a problem does escalate into an issue in the relation, Problem-Solving Skills become very important for the survival of the relation.

188. How Can You Summarize the Effect of the Two-Copartner's Traits in a Relation?

The seven traits of a Copartner, as they relate to being in a relational structure, form an integral part of how a relation works. The Two Copartners are the "engine" of the relation They must both energize their half of the relation in cooperation with their Copartner.

An attracted, committed, genuine, trustworthy, and emotionally mature Copartner, who can communicate and has problem-solving skills, will make positive contributions to any relational structure he or she enters.

Even if the relation must end, a Copartner by way of positive traits will work hard to minimize the harmful emotional and psychological effects.

A Copartner who is not attracted, not committed, not genuine, not trustworthy, and not emotionally mature, who has trouble communicating his or her needs and difficulty with problem-solving skills, will be a challenge in any generic relational structure, to say the least.

189. What are Needs?

Needs, the second subpart used to evaluate a Copartner, provide the motivation each person must have to play his or her role in a relation.

Each Copartner chooses a relational structure based on a personal set of needs. The desire to meet these Needs is why the individual enters the relation in the first place.

Each relational structure in human society has the potential to meet a specific set of needs for its Two Copartners, which is why relational seesaws evolved in the first place, to meet the needs of individuals in a society.

Ideally, each Copartner chooses the seesaw structure that best fulfills the personal needs he/she wants to fulfill.

If you took a group of 50 strangers whose needs were precisely known and grouped them together on an island, you would be able to pick exactly the types of relational structures they would choose and with whom.

190. How Can You Determine All the Needs a Copartner Might Have?

To make things easier to categorize, as with rules, there are four categories of needs.

Learning to use these categories to identify needs will save you hours of wasted time trying to determine what you are missing from your relation. The four categories of Needs are:

- Physical Needs
- Emotional Needs
- Mental Needs
- Social Needs

When you want to be precise for a particular relation, you need to specify the exact PEMS needs that either Copartner might have into one of these four basic categories.

Using these four categories will help you to define and isolate the exact needs each Copartner has and will enable you to determine which relational structure is best suited to meet these needs.

191. What are Some Examples of Physical Needs?

Physical Needs are those involving the body and physiological processes.

Eating, drinking, and sleeping are some examples of personal physical needs that everyone has.

Based on the roles being played by the Copartners, physical needs take different forms.

For example, in a Family relation, the physical needs might involve the home and daily living, such as keeping the living area clean, providing meals for the family, and making sure the home environment is safe and secure.

In the Neighbor/ Neighbor relation physical needs would be entirely different. Here you might have needs for such things as peace and quiet after 10:00 PM, or that your neighbor's leaves don't litter your yard, or for them to return the tools you loaned them two years ago.

Physical needs would also take a different spin in work relations. Here you might have the physical need to keep your workspace clean and organized, make sure safety rules are maintained, or have a comfortable chair for long hours of sitting.

192. What are Some Examples of Emotional Needs?

Emotional Needs are those that mostly involve feelings. The need to be loved, accepted, and nurtured are some examples of personal emotional needs.

In Family relation you would have the emotional need to feel loved, be accepted, and belong to part of the larger group, your family.

Emotional needs are similar in Social relations. You want to feel loved and accepted by your boyfriend or girlfriend. You would like to be able to confide intimate details of your life to your best friend. You would like to feel part of your neighborhood, be invited to block parties, etc.

In Work relations you have a need to be accepted as an equal by your coworkers, be treated with respect by your superiors, and feel part of a bigger whole in the plans of your company.

193. What are Some Examples of Mental Needs?

Mental Needs are those that involve mostly thinking and logic. Curiosity, desire to learn, and the desire to teach new ideas to others are examples of mental needs.

Here, specifically, the nature of the relational structure has a huge impact on the needs of the participants.

For example, if playing the teacher role, he or she would have a need to be organized, present material clearly, and relate his or her teaching to relevant factors in the "real world."

A student would ideally be motivated to learn the subject, or at least be inspired enough to do well on the tests so as to make a good grade in the class.

In a friendship, two people might be inspired to study together or they could be friends who motivate each other in athletic competition. Or perhaps two people both like playing chess, and their friendship is centered on this activity.

In a business, the employer could have a mental need to pass on his/her experience and knowledge to the employees. An employer would also have a strong mental need to train and teach the business expertise to his/her employees which its customers expect to be provided by the company.

194. What are Some Examples of Social Needs?

Social Needs are the needs an individual human has for interacting with other people.

Even though a Copartner is in a one-on-one relation with another person, he/she may want to involve the person from that relation with a wider group of people.

Sharing celebrations, holidays, and meeting with like-minded individuals are some examples of Social Needs.

Social needs in the Family would involve attending other family member's birthdays, sharing family holidays, and/or school holidays.

Social needs for the Social relations involve having someone to share activities with, such as group dating, going to parties, or a neighborhood block party.

At Work, social needs might revolve around the social calendar of the company, perhaps meeting for drinks after work once a week, or attending the educational seminars in your related field.

Social Needs are often linked to the overall group of relations, such as Family, Social, or Work. In other words, Family implies socializing with other families. One Social group of which you are a member might have other social groups they are aligned with. One work group could have social dealings with work groups in the same company or with others in the same vocation.

195. What are Tactics When it Comes to Evaluating the Two Copartners?

Tactics, the third and final subpart that defines how a Copartner interacts in a relation, are the methods and strategic choices used by a person to meet his/her relational needs.

Tactics represent the collection of ways and means that each person uses to meet his or her personal needs in a relation.

The Tactics chosen by each Copartner to meet his/her needs can generally be evaluated as positive or negative. Each Copartner brings a past history of positive and negative tactics to every new relation.

Let's say that a Boss wants an Employee to stay late. A positive Tactic would be to let the Employee know in advance and give him/her an opportunity to rearrange his/her personal schedule.

A negative tactic for meeting the same need would be for the Boss to tell the Employee five minutes before the end of the day that he/she better stay late to finish this project or else be fired.

196. How Do Tactics Give an Insight Into the Two Copartners?

The interesting thing about Tactics is they are often the first sign of trouble in a relation.

Your relation may be going along fine as far as you are concerned, when all of a sudden your Copartner does some weird thing that seems a bit "off." This funny tactic is what triggers you to start wondering, "What's going on here?"

As you start reviewing the incident and working through it in your mind, you realize what happened and the way it happened calls to question the way your Copartner did whatever it was he or she did.

The next step in this process is to go back and review the generic Copartner's Traits, and you will discover whatever it is that you feel uncomfortable about, means your Copartner has some suspect traits.

Were they dishonest, did he or she misrepresent something, does this mean they don't care about you and perhaps are not attracted? By evaluating tactics you actually learn how good your Copartner's Traits are when push comes to shove "on the seesaw."

197. WHY ARE TACTICS SO IMPORTANT ON A RELATIONAL SEESAW?

It's important to pay attention to the Tactics of your Copartner.

The Tactics a Copartner chooses are closely linked to his/her Traits. If a Copartner has positive Traits then he/she will typically use positive Tactics to meet his/her needs within a relation.

A person with positive Traits doesn't feel comfortable attempting to use negative Tactics.

If a Copartner has typically negative Traits, then that person will probably attempt using negative Tactics to meet his/her needs. Often, a person with negative Traits doesn't feel comfortable attempting to use positive Tactics.

This type of person tells a lie when the truth would be easier.

198. What's an Example of a Copartner Using Negative Tactics?

A typical example of negative Traits creating negative Tactics might be an example of a girl we'll call Anne.

Anne has the negative trait of not Being Genuine. She only wants to tell people what she thinks they want to hear. She believes if she does this, people will like her better and she'll get more from a person.

Her friend Lisa calls to see if she wants to go to a movie. Anne is already going to another movie with another friend. Since Anne has a need not to offend Lisa, but since she can't Be Genuine, she just tells Anne that she doesn't want to go. She uses the Tactic of telling Lisa she has a headache.

But her Tactic is negative because she is lying.

Since Anne has the Trait of Not Being Genuine, to her a "little white lie" is "no big deal." And maybe it's not.

But if Anne later goes out for coffee after the movie with a third friend, and happens to run into Jill with other friends, then Anne will have to tell some more lies to explain what happened to her "headache" and how "she tried to call but her phone wasn't working…" as her phone rings exactly at that moment.

This is just one example of how a person with negative Traits combines this with negative Tactics, which can make it very difficult to have a smooth sailing relation.

199. How Can You Summarize the Effect of a Copartner's Tactics?

The ideal Copartners for you in your relation will be the ones who use positive Tactics, as opposed to negative, when trying to meet his or her needs.

Often when evaluating a personal relation, you find that the Environment and the Structure are quite good. But when you analyze the way the relation is going, you find that the other Copartner is using Tactics that conflict with your values.

The tendency is to stick your head in the sand and hope the problem will go away. Unfortunately, negative Tactics and thus Negative Traits, are something that rarely change in a person. If you find yourself on a relational seesaw with this person, it doesn't even matter which one, things generally get worse.

200. So How Can You Evaluate a Copartner Overall?

To define the most complex part of a relation, the Copartner, you will look for the overall combination of his/her Traits, Needs, and Tactics.

Knowing how to evaluate these three subparts allows you to evaluate the specific person with whom you are in a relation, as distinct from the Role that he/she may be playing.

The ability to make this differentiation is crucial to understanding (and evaluating) how well a relation you are involved with is working.

It will take practice for you to grasp the importance and validity of this relation evaluation system. The best way to start is by evaluating all your important relations based on each of the three elements.

As you practice, practice, practice, you will gain a deeper appreciation and understanding of how well your relations are working, as opposed to not evaluating them and hoping for the best.

THE NEXT STEPS TO GENERIC HUMAN STUDIES

WHAT CAN GENERIC HUMAN STUDIES DO FOR ME?

GHS can do a great deal for you.

- It can give you a deeper appreciation of how your body, mind, and relations work.
- It can help you evaluate, diagnose, and manage your body, mind, or relational symptoms.
- It can help you solve the true cause of your body, mind, or relation problems by identifying the actual cause as opposed to a symptomatic flare-up from another area.

You have now been introduced to GHS on an introductory level.

WHAT'S MY NEXT MOVE?

That depends on which area of your life you consider to be your worst problem; your body, your mind, or a relation. A good way to focus inwardly is to ask yourself the following question, "What is my worst problem in life right now?"

Once you decide whether it's a body, mind, or relation problem, continue evaluating your problem using the Generic Human Studies system and this will bring you to a deeper level of understanding your problem. As you learn more about Generic Human Studies®, you can begin to explore its next deeper levels.

About the Author

John K. Pollard, III received his Doctorate of Chiropractic from Los Angeles College of Chiropractic (LACC) in 1976, graduating with distinction.

Subsequently he established and operated one of Southern California's first and most comprehensive wellness and natural therapy clinics, Family Chiropractic Center in Canoga Park, CA.

In 1987, he published SELF-PARENTING: The Complete Guide to Your Inner Conversations, creating the principles and practice of consciously parenting your Inner Child as an Inner Parent.

During this period, he was the featured guest of many radio, news, and television interviews, including CNN; becoming the first chiropractor to create and establish a breakthrough consciousness growth system endorsed and recommended by prominent psychological teachers such as Louise Hay, John Bradshaw, and Ken Keyes, Jr.

www.ingramcontent.com/pod-product-compliance
Ingram Content Group UK Ltd.
Pitfield, Milton Keynes, MK11 3LW, UK
UKHW020132250726
13967UKWH00002B/608